Green Weed

THE
ORGANIC GUIDE
TO GROWING
HIGH-QUALITY
Cannabis

By Dr. Seymour Kindbud

CIDER MILL
PRESS

BOOK
PUBLISHERS

Kennebunkport, ME

13-Digit ISBN: 978-1-60433-157-8
10-Digit ISBN: 1-60433-157-7

LOC Control Number: 2010920333

This book may be ordered by mail from the publisher.
Please include $4.95 for postage and handling.
Please support your local bookseller first!

Books published by Cider Mill Press Book Publishers are
available at special discounts for bulk purchases in the United
States by corporations, institutions, and other organizations. For
more information, please contact the publisher.

Cider Mill Press Book Publishers
"Where good books are ready for press"
12 Port Farm Road
Kennebunkport, Maine 04046

Visit us on the Web!
www.cidermillpress.com

Design by Usana Shadday (www.shadday.com)
Typography: Baskerville, Gil Sans, Marketing Script, & Exquisit
Printed in China

2 3 4 5 6 7 8 9 0

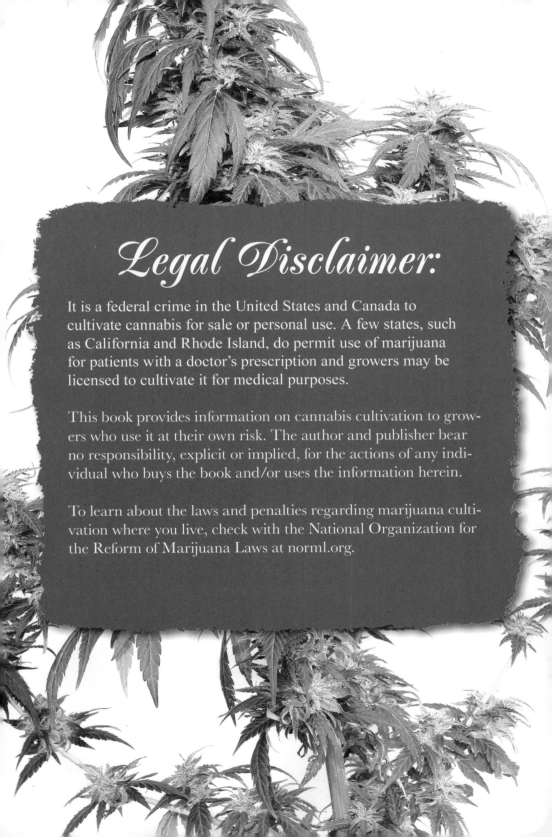

Legal Disclaimer:

It is a federal crime in the United States and Canada to cultivate cannabis for sale or personal use. A few states, such as California and Rhode Island, do permit use of marijuana for patients with a doctor's prescription and growers may be licensed to cultivate it for medical purposes.

This book provides information on cannabis cultivation to growers who use it at their own risk. The author and publisher bear no responsibility, explicit or implied, for the actions of any individual who buys the book and/or uses the information herein.

To learn about the laws and penalties regarding marijuana cultivation where you live, check with the National Organization for the Reform of Marijuana Laws at norml.org.

Table of Contents

CHAPTER ONE

Mother Nature

Grass. Weed. Pot. Ganja. Chronic. The plant known to botanists as *Cannabis* has had a lot of nicknames. One that you don't hear much these days, "Mother Nature," is worth remembering. And not just because of the Beatles' song "Mother Nature's Son," Paul McCartney's ode to the most natural of intoxicants. "Mother Nature" emphasizes what separates marijuana from nearly every other mind-altering substance, from alcohol to cocaine and heroin. It comes straight from nature—no distilling, refining, processing, or manufacturing necessary. It is a product of sunshine, fresh air, and the fertile earth.

Back when people still used the term "Mother Nature," most of the marijuana consumed in the United States was grown in Mexico and Colombia. It was farmed in fields, packed into bricks, hidden in all kinds of inventive ways, and then smuggled into the country with great risk at border crossings. Outside of prime marijuana growing climates such as Northern California, "homegrown" was mostly used as a derogatory term for low-potency, harsh-tasting weed appealing only to those desperate or without connections for the imported varieties.

Much has changed since then. Amateur growers across North America are planting and harvesting for their own use and, with licenses, to supply the medical marijuana clubs that have been legalized in California and Rhode Island. Superb quality homegrown today comes from small outdoor plots or specially lit indoor rooms. Plant breeders—both professionals and hobbyists—have developed strains that thrive in the climate and soil conditions in North America and other varieties with characteristics suited to indoor growing. Breeding has also amped up the potency and productivity, shortened the growing cycle, and enhanced the flavors. "Homegrown" is a slur no more.

Too many growers, however, take the "Mother Nature" out of their homegrown. Whether because of anxiety, greed, or ignorance, a lot of cannabis growers douse their crops with the same chemicals that factory farms dump onto their fields to increase yields, turbocharge plant growth, and kill pests and weeds. These agrichemicals— synthetic fertilizers, pesticides, and herbicides—threaten the health and safety of your family, wildlife, and the environment as a whole. They are highly toxic to people and pets, so they must be handled and stored with extreme caution. And even when used properly, agricultural chemicals (and this includes those used by homeowners on their lawns) are polluting groundwater and harming wildlife. Research has linked them to deformities in frogs and reproductive problems in birds, to cite just a couple of examples of the negative environmental impacts from using chemicals to grow plants. What's worse, too many growers believe that if a little fertilizer or weed-killer is good, more must be better. The excess doesn't even get absorbed by the plants and instead is washed downstream.

Even if you are ready to overlook the risks to the environment, there's a very selfish reason to avoid using chemicals when growing cannabis for your own consumption. Those substances leave behind residues that alter the smell and flavor, giving the smoke an ammonia aftertaste. The overstimulated growth that results from heavy doses of synthetic fertilizers can also water down the weed's natural potency. And I'm not a medical doctor—I earned my degree in weed appreciation—but I've heard lots of anecdotal evidence from regular users who report feeling cramps and aches after smoking marijuana grown with chemicals, symptoms consistent with an excess of toxins in their tissues.

So what's the alternative? The organic approach. Instead of combating Mother Nature, bombing her with one chemical after another all season long, year after year, you work in harmony with the natural processes. You create the conditions in which your plants will thrive, provide for their needs just the same way they've adapted to get them, use smart techniques that mimic nature, and apply only natural products when necessary.

Contrary to what you might believe, you are far more likely to succeed the organic way than if you let your plants develop a chemical dependency. Cannabis is, in many places, a roadside weed, not planted or tended by anyone. So you need to do little more than coax and guide it to maximize its potential. Working against Nature by pumping plants full of chemicals and poisoning all the other living things around them doesn't help them, but rather upsets the balance they've evolved with. Your plants aren't much different than your body—feed it junk food, load up on steroids, don't get enough exercise or sleep, and you will in the end be sick and not able to perform your best.

The benefits are worth the effort. Ask any of the leading chefs or winemakers and they'll tell you that organic ingredients taste best. The goal of this book is to help you succeed at growing your own healthy and pure, tasty and potent, patch of pot. And when you're done, you'll feel right that you didn't pollute the environment or load your harvest up with chemicals that could harm you and ruin the flavor of your homegrown. Whether you have harvested many buds before or never planted a single seed, you can use this book's simple instructions for choosing the right strain, building perfect soil, planting, care and maintenance, harvesting, and problem-solving to raise your own

crop of truly green weed. This information comes from my years of experience raising all kinds of plants organically and from the veteran marijuana growers I consulted as I researched this book.

I can think of no better way to honor Mother Nature than to enjoy a little organic homegrown outside on a fine day. Ready to join me? Let's dig in!

CHAPTER TWO

What's In The Names?

Brand names have long been part of the marijuana marketplace. Back in the day, dealers and users talked up their Panama Red, Acapulco Gold, and Maui Wowie. Today, you hear about new names almost daily, but some of the best known and most highly coveted current brands are Kush, Sour Diesel, AK-47, and Blueberry.

Do those names mean anything? Well, dealers still hype their wares by dropping the names of desirable varieties. But the names really are grounded in plant breeding and understanding them can help you be more successful as a grower.

Let's start with a little science talk. *Cannabis* is the genus of the marijuana plant. (Remember: All living things are classified by domain, kingdom, phylum, class, order, family, genus, and species.) There are four species in the genus: *Cannabis sativa*, *Cannabis indica*, *Cannabis afghanica* and *Cannabis ruderalis*. Each of these species have developed a number of "strains," which vary because they've adapted to the different conditions in which they've been grown.

So when talking about different strains, plant breeders assess the different qualities of each one, from when it flowers to how many buds it produces, its tolerance for heat and drought, its potency and flavor, and much more. When creating new strains, breeders use simple techniques that people have used with plants for centuries, starting with selecting the best specimens in each crop that have desired characteristics, then saving and planting their seeds. Breeders also hand-pollinate between two species to blend their desirable qualities.

When a plant breeder creates a new plant hybrid—whether it's tomato, corn, or cannabis—they can give it a "cultivar" name because it is a distinct plant with unique qualities. Kush, Silver Haze, Sour Diesel, and other cannabis brand names are like Big Beef tomato or Silver Queen corn. So, to the degree that you know where your buds come from and can trust the grower or dealer, the names are meaningful. And when you grow, knowing the qualities of the varieties you have to choose from can help you get the best for your needs.

Sativa vs. Indica

Cannabis sativa and *indica* are the most potent species of cannabis and they have adapted to a wide range of climates and conditions. The two species each have distinct qualities. Sativa is native (meaning it grows in the wild) in Mexico, Central America, Colombia, and Jamaica, as well as Thailand and other areas close to the equator. It was the most widely available type of cannabis until the early 1980s. Sativa is very potent because of its high content of THC (tetrahydrocannabinol), the alkaloid that creates the sensation of being high. Its flavors and scents tend to be earthy and faintly sweet. Those who have compared the two species report that sativas seem to have a stimulant effect, relieving migraines and, because it stirs up your appetite, nausea.

Sativa plants grow up tall and thin, with narrow, light green leaves. Sativa plants grow very quickly and can get to 20 feet tall

during a normal season. The buds develop with yellowish pigments to protect them from intense light, but they mature to a more reddish hue (even closer to purple in cooler climates). They are comparatively slow to mature, taking three to four months after flowering to be ready for harvesting. Sativas tend to produce fewer buds than indica varieties.

The indicas are native in regions such as Afghanistan, Kashmir, Morocco, and Turkey, and were developed primarily for making hashish, the balls and cakes made from gummy cannabis resin that have long been smoked in a hookah in traditional Middle Eastern cafes and homes. Indica's effects tend toward relaxation, making it helpful for relieving anxiety, pain, muscle spasms, and sleep disorders.

Indica plants are shorter, denser than sativas with broad, dark-green leaves. They grow faster and mature more quickly—they're often ready to harvest two months after flowering begins. The typical indica scent is pungent and "skunky," and the taste often hints at fruit and pine.

Choosing A Variety

The best variety for you to grow depends on a number of factors. Of course, which you have access to is most likely to determine which you grow. But if you have choices, consider these general guidelines before making your selection.

Outdoors or In? The height, slow growth, and long maturation period of sativas make them best for growing outside. If you are growing inside, the shorter plants and quicker life cycle of indicas make them more manageable.

Warm or Cool? If you live where spring warms up quickly and the summers are long and hot, sativas will thrive in your conditions. Indicas are a better choice in cooler climates with shorter growing seasons.

Open or Discreet? Towering sativa plants attract more attention, especially late in the season when most other plants are turning brown and dying down. Go for indicas if you need to keep your plot out of sight.

Quality or Quantity? If your goal is to grow the best-tasting, most potent buds, plant sativas. You get more buds with stronger (some say harsher) flavor from indicas.

Perfect Balance

Most of the widely-distributed varieties are hybrids of the two species, each with different qualities selected and bred into them from the pure strains. As much as you can, find out about the qualities of the hybrids you're considering and choose one that is best adapted to your conditions. Plants growing in the right conditions need much less attention and are far less prone to problems than those out of their element.

No matter where you are growing, you dramatically increase your chances for success if you can plant several different varieties. This protects you from complete failure if one variety is not well-adapted to your conditions. It can also extend the duration of your harvest as each variety may mature at a slightly different time.

Most important for your long-term success, planting different varieties in your first years of growing allows you to compare the performance of each. Once you see which variety handles your conditions best and yields buds that suit your tastes, you can focus your future efforts on it. Even more valuable, if you allow some of your best plants to bear seeds and you replant those seeds the following season, you will, in a few years, have a strain you've developed on your own that is perfectly adapted to your environment.

QUICK HITS

- Brand names can be just hype, but they also help growers choose the right strain for their needs.
- Plant sativas outside, indicas indoors.
- Grow a few different varieties, especially when you are a newbie.

A tip from Dr. Kindbud: Ask experienced growers in your area which varieties grow best for them. The top choices in Northern California or British Columbia may not be ideal for your conditions.

Cannabis Cup

Competitive weed breeding? That's the stated purpose of the Cannabis Cup, which is held in Amsterdam during the week of Thanksgiving each year. And it's true that the top cannabis breeders from around the world bring their buds to be evaluated, rated, and perhaps awarded prizes for the best new varieties and the coveted cup. The competition also presents a unique opportunity for any weed-lover willing to pay for a "judge's pass" (about $200 in 2009) to sample the finest varieties found anywhere.

Launched in 1987 by the editor of *High Times* magazine, the Cannabis Cup is awarded in five different categories, including prizes for the best sativa and indica varieties, and hash. A panel of invited expert judges determines the winner of the breeding awards, while the "judges-at-large" (purchasers of the judge's pass)" vote on winners in other categories, such as best glass pipes and best accessory or product.

Along with the competition, the event has now become a weeklong celebration of all things ganja. It features concerts by well-known performers, booths full of products for growers and users, and the induction ceremony for the "Counterculture Hall of Fame." If you plan to be a serious grower and you have the means to get to this weedfest, you're sure to pick up lots of valuable information— and have a real good time.

Past winners of the Cannabis Cup:

1988 - Skunk #1
1989 - Early Pearl/Skunk #1 x Northern Lights #5/Haze
1990 - Northern Lights #5 4th Cup
1991 - Skunk from Free City
1992 - Haze x Skunk #1
1993 - Haze x Northern Lights #5
1994 - Jack Herer
1995 - White Widow
1996 - White Russian
1997 - Peace Maker
1998 - Super Silver Haze
1999 - Super Silver Haze
2000 - Blueberry
2001 - Sweet Tooth
2002 - Morning Glory
2003 - Hawaiian Snow
2004 - Amnesia Haze
2005 - Willie Nelson
2006 - Arjan's Schoenmaker Zwervers Ultra Haze #1
2007 - G-13 Haze
2008 - Super Lemon Haze

CHAPTER THREE

Going Underground

The key to successfully growing any plant—whether it's a 300-foot-tall redwood tree, a tomato vine heavy with fruit, or bud-laden stalks of marijuana—is under your feet. In the right soil, nearly every plant will grow up healthy and productive with little care, and in poor soil no chemical, potion, or TLC can help the plant overcome it. As an organic grower, your mission is to ensure that the soil where you are planting your cannabis crop is just right for its needs.

The right soil for growing marijuana, or just about any other crop, is "biologically active." Consider this fact: there are more living organisms in a teaspoon of healthy soil than there are people on Earth. That's right, healthy soil is teeming with billions of microscopic bacteria and fungi. They break down organic matter—the remains of decayed leaves, stems, and roots—and turn it into nutrients plants feed on. Over millions of years, plants evolved in a co-dependent relationship with these microbes. An organic grower focuses on nurturing a robust population of soil microbes so they can support the plants' growth.

Good Dirt

Soil in most places is a mix of sand (or finely ground rock) and clay, along with organic matter. Perfectly balanced soil is known as "loam" and if that naturally occurs where you are, you are very fortunate (and farming is likely a popular occupation in your area). Far more common is soil that is predominantly either clay or sand (especially in coastal areas).

Clay soil tends to be dense and hard-packed, making it tough for plants' roots to spread out and for water to saturate the area around the roots. It also has no room for air pockets, which the microbes and roots must have. In contrast, sandy soil is loose and very porous, so water and nutrients drain away quickly, before the microbes and roots can absorb them. While you can't completely transform the soil's basic make-up, you can bring it closer to balance. Adding organic matter to the soil—I'll explain how further along in this chapter—helps to loosen heavy clay soil and gives sandy soil a way to hold onto moisture until it is needed. It is also the fuel the microbes need to stay active and nourish your plants.

The soil's water-holding capacity, often referred to as "drainage," is critical to plants' health. Of course, you probably already realize that plants take up water through their roots. They do this gradually, so they need time for that. But not too much time. When the soil is water-logged, the plants' roots can suffer from rot and may even drown (when the air pockets in soil fill up with water, the plants literally drown for a lack of air). You can test the soil's drainage easily with the "Percolation Test" explained on page 38.

The ABCs of pH

Another important soil attribute you need to be aware of is its pH. Forgive me if this causes unpleasant flashbacks from your high school science classes, but it will help you to understand what pH is and how it affects plants.

An abbreviation for "potential hydrogen," pH measures the amount of positively charged hydrogen ions (H+) versus negatively charged hydroxide ions (OH) in a solution (soil, for example). A solution with a neutral pH has a balanced amount of hydrogen and hydroxide ions. The higher the concentration of hydrogen ions, the more acidic or "sweet" the soil is. Where hydroxide ions dominate, the soil becomes alkaline, which is also described as "basic" or "sour." The system used to measure pH is based on a scale that ranges from 0.0 (most acidic) to 14.0 (most alkaline), with 7.0 being neutral. Each unit on the pH scale represents a tenfold difference in acidity or alkalinity. For example, soil with a pH of 5.0 is 100 times more acidic than neutral soil.

What does this chemistry lesson have to do with your plants? Nutrients must dissolve in the soil-and-water solution for plants to absorb them, and the pH of soil significantly affects the solubility of minerals. Where soil pH is below 6.0, the key macronutrients of nitrogen, phosphorus, and potassium are less accessible to plants. In soil with a pH above 7.5, plants cannot access essential nutrients like iron, manganese, and phosphorus. The ideal pH for cannabis plants is slightly acidic, from 6.3 to 6.8.

Testing, Testing

Now that you know what your pH needs to be, let's get into how you measure it. That is, soil testing. You can buy home soil test kits that are easy to use and relatively accurate. In most cases, however, the only reading they typically give you is pH. The "land-grant" university in every U.S. state (such as Cornell in New York and Texas A&M) is required to offer low-cost soil tests to farmers and home gardeners, as do many private laboratories around the country and in Canada. You can find your local soil-testing laboratories online or contact your county's cooperative extension service (every county has one), which will be listed in the blue "government" pages of the phone book.

Lab soil tests measure not only pH, they also assess the levels of potassium, phosphorus, calcium, and other major nutrients—nitrogen is the exception, because it changes so rapidly in soil that any one-time measure of it will not be useful. The tests also measure the soil's organic matter level (5 percent is ideal) and check for the presence of damaging heavy metals, including lead and arsenic. Today's most sophisticated labs go even further, measuring the soil's level of biological activity.

Soil test results typically include advice on how to remedy pH imbalances and nutrient deficiencies. This information can be very useful to you, but bear in mind that the recommendations are most often not organic, unless specified. Look at your soil test report as an indication of the direction you want to go rather than as a road map to follow.

Organic Matter Rules

The most important reading on your soil test, and a critical and often overlooked component of the soil where you will grow your crop is organic matter. As I mentioned, it is the residue of decaying leaves, stems, and other parts of plants. In forests, meadows, and most every environment where plants grow naturally, organic matter is a basic building block of soil, created as plants die, fall to the ground, and decompose. The dead and decaying plants are consumed by worms and all the less visible creatures in the soil's food chain. In this process, the nutrients the dead plants consumed are transformed back into nutrients that living plants can absorb.

If organic matter only nourished your plants and the microbes in the soil, it would be very valuable. But organic matter is so essential because it also remedies the weaknesses of both clay and sandy soils. It helps break up heavy clay soil, as earthworms tunnel through to get to the rotting plants they feed on. Sandy soils need the nutrients that are slowly released as the organic matter decays. All types of soil benefit from the way organic matter absorbs water and then gradually disperses it.

It is possible to have too much organic matter in the soil, but practically that is hard to do because its nature is to constantly decay. That's why you want to continuously add organic matter to your soil, no matter if it's mostly clay, sand, or loam. The good news is that the resources you need to replenish the organic matter in your soil are free and lying on the ground outside your door. Leaves and grass clippings work exceptionally well for this purpose. If possible, shred the leaves first with a bagging lawn mower to get them started on decomposing. (Earthworms, by the way, are voracious consumers of leaves, and after eating they deposit their nutrient-rich poop in the soil.) With grass clippings, be sure they come from a lawn that has not been treated with herbicides, synthetic fertilizer, or other chemicals. Mix a couple inch layer of organic matter into your soil before planting. And throughout the growing season, keep your soil blanketed with a 2 to 4 inch layer of leaves and/or grass clippings. After your harvest, work

more organic matter into the top few inches of the soil to begin decomposing over the dormant months.

Crazy for Compost

The easiest way to add organic matter to your soil is by putting on that layer of mulch like I just described. The best way to build your soil's organic matter, though, is with compost. Organic farmers and gardeners call compost "black gold," because it is invaluable to growing any crop. It provides a balanced array of nutrients, and it also tends to be slightly acidic, so it helps to get the pH right for your cannabis crop. Compost works like a sponge in the soil, absorbing moisture when it is available and then gradually dispersing it as the soil dries. Last but far from least, compost is loaded with a high concentration of beneficial microbes which are not only ready to begin digesting other organic matter in the soil but also have been proven to combat the nasty soil organisms that cause plant diseases.

Sounds miraculous, doesn't it? Even more amazing, compost is incredibly easy to make using ingredients you already have on hand. It's also, by the way, a very basic act of environmental responsibility because when you make compost you reduce the volume of garbage you put in the waste stream.

You can find detailed instructions for making compost online, but let me give you the basics right here. Start by finding a spot that is no less than 3 feet wide and 3 feet long. Spread a layer of fallen leaves or straw (not hay, which contains weed seeds) on the ground. Top that with a layer of grass clippings from your lawn, kitchen scraps from fruits and vegetables (like banana peels and the tops of carrots). You can also toss in spent plants from your yard and garden, dead houseplants, and the like. Whenever you have this kind of waste, keep adding it to the pile. Include both brown material (dry, dead stuff) and green (fresh, damp stuff). If you don't have enough all at once, no problem—just add it as you get it.

I made a list for you of all the things you can and must not put in your compost pile (see "Compost Yeas and Nays" on page 41). Just bear in mind that a compost pile produces the best fertilizer and soil conditioner for your plants when you add three parts brown stuff to every one part green stuff. (Too much brown stuff and the pile will decompose too slowly; too much green stuff and it will get mucky and may smell bad.) The ratios don't have to be exact at all times—you can add what you have when you have it. If the ingredients are very dry, moisten but don't soak the pile. One ingredient you don't need is the compost starter or "inoculant" sold in nurseries and online. Many studies have found that they make no difference in the compost's quality or how quickly it is produced. Save your money.

Once the pile is about 3 feet high, decomposition will speed up to the point where you can see the changes. Every other week or so, use a shovel or a garden fork to move the stuff in the center of the pile—which will be warm and visibly decomposed—to the outside and move the uncomposted matter to the center. If you keep this up, in about three to five months the center of the pile will look like chocolate cake crumbs (the original ingredients now unrecognizable) and smell earthy and kind of sweet. Congratulations—you've got compost!

Want to jack up the nutrient levels in your compost and speed the process? All you need is poultry manure. Sounds gross, I know, but manure from chickens or turkeys is like concentrated nitrogen, which will send the decomposers in your compost pile into a feeding frenzy, with enough left behind to turbocharge your plants' growth. Manure from cows, sheep, and horses works, too, but isn't as "hot" or as nitrogen-rich. If you live near a farm, get yourself a container with a secure lid and ask if you can scoop up a bin full of animal waste—straw or other bedding included. It'll be worth enduring the stink when you see your plants grow strong and productive.

You don't need a special compost bin but if you want to keep the pile looking neat, you can buy a variety of models that look tidy and make it easy to turn the ingredients and remove the compost when it is finished. Or you can make a simple but effective bin with discarded wooden pallets and chicken wire. Many municipalities trying to reduce their wastestream also now provide basic compost bins to residents. Check to see if yours does.

To get the maximum benefits of your homemade compost, you want to use it strategically. First, work some into the soil when you are preparing a new bed. Add it about 4 to 6 weeks before planting. This give the beneficial microbes time to move out of the compost and into the surrounding soil, where they can begin processing the organic matter already there. If you are planting seeds directly in the ground outdoors, mix a half-inch or so into the seedbed just before sowing. For transplants, toss a couple handfuls of compost into each hole and work it into the soil where it will get your seedlings off to a strong start.

One more invaluable use for compost: if you are starting or growing your crop in containers, the soil mixes you buy for that come with either synthetic fertilizers already in them (look for blue or green crystals) or no nutrients at all. To keep your crop pure, you want the mix with no nutrients. Instead, mix finished compost into the soil mix.

Booster Shots

Compost can work wonders for your soil, but it takes a few months to be ready to use. And if your soil has more serious deficiencies, you may need more powerful remedies. The following all-natural soil "amendments" can help make fast changes.

Too acidic: Powdered lime, especially from finely ground oyster shells or limestone.
Too alkaline: Elemental sulfur. If your soil test also shows low levels of potassium and magnesium, look for products labeled as Sul-Po-Mag.
Low nitrogen: Blood meal (aka dried blood), fish meal, feather meal, composted poultry manure (sold in pellets).
Low phosphorus: Colloidal or rock phosphate.
Low potassium: Greensand, wood ash, or seaweed.
Low calcium: Bonemeal, oyster shell lime.
Excessive clay: Agricultural gypsum.

Be sure to follow the application instructions carefully. Adding too much of one element can make other key nutrients inaccessible to your plants. When it comes to getting your soil right, don't fall into the trap of believing that if a little is good, a lot is better.

Till or Not

Before we leave the topic of soil building and care, I want to take a moment to address the practice of mechanically tilling the soil. When turning an uncultivated plot into a planting bed for the first time, a power tiller is a very handy tool. It can break up sod or other plant cover, and a tiller loosens soil quickly and easily. It is no more effective than working with a spade, but less work.

But some growers, especially those who have bought a power tiller, use the machine every year to prep their planting beds and often pull it out periodically during the growing season to cultivate weeds between rows. All studies of this practice have found that in the long term it turns the soil in to dust and harms earthworms and other soil-dwelling creatures. So, if you want to rent a tiller to build your bed for the first time, go right ahead. But in future seasons and when you have weeds to eliminate, stick with hand tools.

QUICK HITS

- Get your soil tested before adding anything to it.
- Add organic matter regularly, especially compost.
- Use organic soil amendments for serious deficiencies.
- Don't till repeatedly.
- Check your soil's drainage. It should be 1 to 4 inches per hour.

A tip from Dr. Kindbud: Gather and store grass clippings and leaves when they are plentiful (spring and summer for the former, autumn for the latter) so you'll have them on hand as you need them throughout the season.

Pass The Percolation Test

Use this easy test to see how quickly water percolates (or drains) in your plot's soil.

1. Dig three or fours holes in various spots in the area where you intend to plant your crop. Each hole should be about 1½ feet deep and at least 6 inches wide.

2. Pour water into the holes after digging, and wait until it all has drained away. Then fill the hole with water to the top again.

3. The next day, come back and fill the holes with water again. Then check regularly to see how long before the water drains away:

• Less than a half inch in an hour indicates poor drainage.
• One half to 1 inch per hour is slow but acceptable.
• 1 to 4 inches in an hour is ideal for most plants, including cannabis.
• Faster than 4 inches in an hour shows that the soil holds too little moisture.

Compost Yeas And Nays

Yes

Kitchen scraps from fruits and vegetables,
e.g. broccoli stems and banana peels
Leaves, flowers, stalks, and other parts of dead
garden and house plants
Grass clippings (not from chemically treated lawns)
Straw (but not hay)
Egg shells
Coffee grounds and tea bags
Shredded paper (moderate amounts)
Wood ash (moderate amounts)
Manure from herbivores, including cows, sheep,
chickens, rabbits, and guinea pigs
Hair from salons, barber shops, and pet groomers

No

Meat scraps
Oil and oil-soaked paper
Manure from dogs, cats, people, or other carnivores

CHAPTER FOUR

Making Your Bed

In the last chapter, I emphasized the importance of soil-building to growing the best possible crop of organic cannabis. That's an ongoing effort from before you plant to after the last harvest. But if you're just starting out or planning to grow in a new location, you'll want to know how to transform a plot of ground into a bed ready for you to plant in.

You have two choices: the slow, lazy way or the fast, hard approach. I'll explain both. But first, let's go over what to look for when choosing the best location for your plot.

The Ideal Location. You won't find a better site than a south-facing slope (picture a vineyard) with a wide variety of wild flowers and a few very tall trees on it.

However, if this isn't in the cards for you, look for...

Full sun. To grow up strong and produce lots of buds, cannabis plants need at least 10 hours of sunlight each day. Site your bed where it won't be shaded by buildings, fences, or dense short trees, shrubs, or other plants (sunlight filters down from very tall trees). If the only options you have are shaded at least part of the day, go for one that gets afternoon sun, which lasts into the evening during the height of summer, as opposed to morning sun. Generally, beds facing south or west get the most light.

<u>Shelter from artificial lights.</u> While your plants need lots of sunlight, as I'll explain in detail in Chapter 6, you want your plot shielded from street lights and other artificial lights.

<u>Not too wet.</u> The last chapter explained the importance of the soil's ability to drain water, how to assess it, and improve it, but no amount of work you put in can overcome a location that traps and holds water. Don't plant in very low-lying or swampy areas—your crop will drown there. Also, be wary of locations close to creeks, ponds, and other bodies of water that could overflow. The soil there is likely to be very fertile, but cannabis cannot tolerate flooding.

<u>The right size.</u> You can make your whole plot as big as you want, but break it up into a series of beds about 4 feet wide and 8 to 10 feet long, with pathways on all sides of each of them. This size lets you reach into the beds—to water or pull weeds—from

one side or another without stepping on the soil, which can compress it and squeeze out all the pockets where water and air move through. The pathways can be left in grass or other low-growing plants or covered with wood chips, if you prefer.

Slow and Easy

The easiest method for turning uncultivated ground into a planting bed is also the best way. That's because you will be building the soil at the same time you are transforming it. But you need at least three to four months and the following supplies:

Paper. Sheets of black-and-white newsprint (no colored ink, which may contain heavy metals, or glossy paper, which breaks down too slowly). Get about eight sheets for every square foot of bed you plan to make. If you prefer, you can use kraft paper, which is the thicker type used for paper grocery bags, or cardboard. You need only one layer of those on each bed.

Peat moss. You can buy it in big bags at home stores and garden centers. Get enough to cover each bed about 3 to 4 inches thick. (You may have heard that bogs and other natural habitats are threatened by peat moss harvesting. That is true in the United Kingdom, but Canadian sphagnum peat moss is managed sustainably according to the strict rules of Canada's government.)

Organic matter. Grass clippings, straw (not hay, which often contains weed seeds) and shredded leaves. If you have access to animal manure (cow, chicken, or sheep), get as much of that as you can. Be sure the grass clippings do not come from a lawn that is treated with chemical fertilizers and herbicides.

Start by spreading a layer of the paper or cardboard on top of the ground. That's right, you're not going to dig at all or bother removing the plants that are already growing there. Instead, you will simply smother them. Be sure the sheets of paper overlap each other, so no sunlight gets through to the ground.

Top the paper with an inch or two of peat moss and blanket that with an equally thick layer of the organic matter. Continue alternating layers of peat and organic matter until you've used up all you have.

Now you can kick back and relax. Your work is done. In 12 to 16 weeks, the layers will have decomposed, blended together, and wiped out any vegetation growing on the spot. When you're ready to plant, just dig through the layers and make holes. This approach works best if you cover the soil with the layers in fall and then plant in it the following spring.

Faster, Harder

Can't wait three months or more to start planting? With a little muscle and sweat, or a powerful machine, you can prepare the bed and plant the same day. You will need:

Spade or carpet knife. A spade is a hand tool that looks like a shovel but has a straight, sharp edge at the bottom. A carpet knife is a blade used by people who install flooring.

Shovel or garden fork. A shovel has a point at the end and works best when it is sharp. A garden fork has a few wide, pointed tines (in contrast to the manure or compost fork, which has many thin, pointed tines).

A gas-powered tiller. If you have this, you don't need the other tools. You can rent one from many hardware stores or rental shops or you may be able to borrow one from a gardener/farmer you trust. You want a rear-tine tiller rather than a front-tine type, which generally don't have the power you need to break up grass or hard-packed soil easily.

A rake. Use a hard-tined garden rake, not a soft-tined leaf rake. After marking the perimeter of your plot with stakes and string or a garden hose, you can run the tiller through the area at least twice, then use the rake to pull out large chunks of plants and their roots. Don't obsess about getting rid of every little bit. Smaller pieces decompose quickly and add valuable organic matter to the soil. Break up any large clods of soil you see either with the rake or your hands.

If you have no tiller, the spade or carpet knife let you slice into and peel back the top layer of vegetation on the soil. With the spade, go around the perimeter of your planting area and jab it into the soil about 3 inches deep. (This is where having the sharp edge is critical.) Then work around the bed in 3 by 3 foot sections, pushing the spade back into the soil then moving it as vertically as possible to get underneath the roots of whatever is growing there and lifting it. As you separate each section, shake it over the bed so that any loose soil falls back onto it. If a lot of soil is clumped to the bottom of the section you remove, use your fingers to break it free and put it back onto the now exposed ground.

Use the carpet knife just like you were removing an old rug. While on your hands and knees, slice through the vegetation layer with the knife to about that same depth of 3 inches or so. With your fingers, peel back each section and remove as much loose soil from it as you can before you gather up the removed pieces and put them in your compost pile.

After you've used the spade or the knife to remove the sod or other ground-covering plants, work the shovel or fork into the soil and loosen it down to about 12 inches (if that's not possible, go as deep as you can). Remove any large stones. Mix organic matter, such as grass clippings, dry leaves, straw, peat, or, best of all, compost, into the top six inches of the soil.

Your bed is now ready to plant. Whether you used a tiller, spade, or carpet knife, you want to do all you can to avoid stepping on the planting area ever again. When you walk on soil, you compact it, which squeezes out air pockets that are essential for letting oxygen and water reach the plants' roots.

Remember to keep a mulch layer of organic matter on the top of the soil throughout the growing season. Add more after the season is over and if you keep doing this, your bed will get more fertile from one year to the next.

QUICK HITS

• The easy way to prepare a bed is to layer the ground with weed-blocking newspaper and top that with piles of organic matter. Wait four months to plant.
• The fast way to prepare a bed is to remove the sod or other ground cover with a tiller, spade, or carpet knife. Mix organic matter into the soil and plant that day.
• Make your beds four feet wide by eight to 10 feet long.
• Never walk on your plot after you've prepared it.

A tip from Dr. Kindbud: Never work in soil that is muddy. It will clump up and become too hard for roots to penetrate.

Raising The Bed

The best possible conditions for growing your cannabis crop is in a raised bed. By elevating the planting area six inches or more above the ground:

- You can plant earlier in spring, because the soil warms up and dries out faster.
- Your plants can spread their roots out in loose soil.
- You can concentrate your soil-building effort right where it's needed most.
- You never need to walk on the bed, so the soil stays loose and full of air pockets.

Making a raised bed is easy. Add as much compost as you can and mix in other soil amendments to the area where you will plant. Then use a rake to scrape soil up from the pathways into a mound about four feet wide. When the mound is at least six inches high, use your rake to level it off.

Many organic gardeners frame their raised beds to make them look neater and to slow their erosion. If you want to do this, you can build a frame out of wood - just be sure it's not "pressure-treated" lumber or old railroad ties, both of which can leach heavy metals into the soil and spoil your organic crop. Cedar is a naturally rot-resistant wood, which is expensive but lasts a long time. Ordinary, untreated lumber works fine and lasts more than five years. You can also use recycled plastic lumber, often sold in hardware stores under the brand name "Trex." Bricks or large stones work for framing raised beds, too. You can also buy raised bed kits online.

A bed without a frame will erode during the growing season. But if you use every square inch of the bed to plant in, even the sides, the roots will hold the soil in place.

CHAPTER FIVE

Starting Up

You have a few choices to make when starting your cannabis crop. First, will you grow from seeds or cuttings (or clones) taken from existing plants? If you've never grown before, the answer to the question may depend on which of those you have access to. Do you know an existing grower with a healthy, good quality crop who is willing to share a few starts with you? (If you already are growing and are reading this book to make the switch to a more natural and sustainable approach, you can use cuttings from your existing crop and simply use organic care going forward.)

Seed Viability

Without access to already started plants or clones, you will have to plant seeds. You can just gather seeds from all the good buds you smoke and ask your friends to save theirs, too. Before long you'll have the few dozen you need to plant a manageable size crop. You can also buy seeds from online sources—check the "Resources" section in the back of this book for a few links.

Before you plant seeds, take the time to check their viability, or their readiness to grow. In general, the ones that are dark, round, and feel solid are viable, and any that are pale or white, dented or crushed in any way, or seem light in weight are not. You can quickly check their viability by pouring them all into a bowl of water. Those that float are at least partially hollow and will not sprout. The sinkers are ready for planting.

If the seeds are kind of old or if you have any other doubts about them, take the time to do a sprouting test. Moisten a paper towel, place a few seeds on it, roll it up, and place it in a resealable plastic bag. After three days, take the paper towel out, carefully unroll it and look to see if the seeds have sprouted—they'll have tiny white rootlets coming out. If none have sprouted, reroll it and put it back in the bag. Check again each day for the next ten, making sure the towel remains damp (moisten it lightly if it has dried out). After two weeks, you should see that some have sprouted. If not, you need to get a new supply of seeds.

Outdoors or In?

When you have a supply of viable seeds, you are ready for the next decision. You can plant them directly in the ground outside or start them inside in "seedling" trays and then transplant them outside when they are established and the weather is hospitable.

Sowing the seeds directly in the soil outside is the least amount of work and is safest if you don't want to have cannabis plants in your home. But you have to wait until the nighttime temperatures are warm enough (60 degrees Fahrenheit) and you need to plant a lot of extra seeds to compensate for those that fail to germinate and that you lose to birds and other animals. Starting indoors does not require expensive equipment, but does take time and attention. In return, you get a longer growing season because the plants are more mature when the weather warms enough for them to go outside. Bigger, more mature plants produce more buds and they're more potent. And you are more likely to succeed with transplants than with seeds, because plants started indoors have already passed their most vulnerable stage.

Direct to the Ground

I'll explain both processes for you, starting with what farmers and gardeners call "direct sowing," or planting seeds right in the ground. The basic steps are no different, whether you are growing cannabis or corn.

Just sprouted plants won't tolerate the chills, so you want to know the last frost date for your area. Your county—every county—has an extension office for the state's "land grant" university (find it online or in the blue pages of the phone book). The office provides information to farmers and gardeners, and can tell you the average last frost date where you live.

About three weeks before your last frost date, rake or cultivate the top few inches of the soil in your plot to remove any weeds, clumps of soil, or large stones. Check it a few more times as your frost date nears and pull any weeds that come up. When you rake the soil, you bring to the surface weed seeds lurking underground. You want them to germinate so you can get rid of them before they compete with your crop.

Plant your seeds as soon as you can after your last frost date. Just be sure to wait until the ground is not muddy from melting snow or spring rain. Right before you plant, spread a half-inch to an inch of compost on the soil. Use a hand shovel or a hoe to carve out a furrow (or shallow trench) about an inch deep. It can be as long as your bed allows.

Lightly moisten, but don't soak the soil. Watering before rather than after planting the seeds protects them from being swamped, or washed up and out of the soil.

Spread the seeds down the furrow about 3 to 5 inches apart. Gently press each of them into the soil to be sure they have contact

with it. Replace the soil you dug out on top of the seeds. Firm the soil on top but don't pack it down so hard that the sprouts can't come through it.

The soil must be kept consistently damp so that when the seeds sprout and put out their first roots, they have water available. Without it, they could come up and then die very quickly, within just a few hours on a warm, sunny day. Lightly sprinkle water on the seedbed whenever it's dry on the surface until the seeds have sprouted. When you see the little sprouts poking up, spread dried grass clippings, shredded fall leaves, or straw on the surface of the soil all around them. A 1 to 2 inch layer of these organic mulches keeps the soil from drying out too quickly and it blocks sunlight from any weed seeds that might have landed on the exposed soil.

I'll explain in upcoming chapters how to care for your sprouts once they've come up. Right now, I'm going to tell you how to start seeds indoors.

Indoor Start

Planting your seeds indoors and then transplanting them outside after they've grown in a protected environment for a month or two is the best way to grow in any climate. The plants get a head start on the growing season, so they grow bigger and bushier before they start making buds. More mature plants are better able to withstand weather extremes and are less inviting to deer, rabbits, and other plant-eating wildlife. Perhaps most important if you are trying to avoid drawing attention to your plot, you don't have to check on and water larger plants daily as you do with sprouts that have just come up from seeds.

The equipment you need to start seeds indoors is inexpensive and available at nurseries, hardware stores, and home centers.

Fluorescent shop lights. A four-bulb fixture is best, but a two-bulb unit works fine. Get an equal number of "warm" and "cool" bulbs.

Seedling trays. These are rectangular plastic trays containing removable plastic planting cells. Vegetable and flower gardeners pick these up in nurseries and from online sources in late winter and early spring. You may see seed-starting kits with "automatic" watering that promise to make your seeds more successful. You can use them, but they are not necessary.

Soil-less mix. The soil from outside or even potting mix you can buy for houseplants holds too much moisture and is too heavy for starting seeds inside. Soil-less mix is a blend of peat moss or coir (a sustainable product made of the fibers leftover from coconut processing) and either perlite or vermiculite, which are minerals mined and heated so they can hold and disperse water gradually. Soil-less mix often is sold with synthetic fertilizers added to the mix—pass on those for your organic cannabis crop. You can blend your own mix by buying the raw ingredients in bulk or just pick up a few bags at your local nursery in late winter or early spring.

Compost. If you have not made your own yet (but you will, right?), you can buy a small bag at a nursery.

Dr. Kindbud's Pro Tool Kit

Spear and Jackson tools: Shovels, spades, rakes, forks, and trowels made with high-quality steel, hardwood handles, and true craftsmanship. www.spear-and-jackson.com

Cobrahead Weeder and Cultivator: A tool that works like a giant fingernail, making quick, easy work of carving open a furrow, loosening soil, levering out deep-rooted weeds and more. www.cobrahead.com

Felco pruners: Carbon steel blades that stay sharp, ergonomically designed grips, a reliable latch, and replaceable parts make these the choice of nearly every professional and serious amateur gardener. www.felcostore.com

Haws watering can: Perfectly balanced and with a long neck so you can pour the water exactly where you want it to go. www.hawswateringcans.com

Atlas Fit Garden Gloves: The rubber coating on the palms and fingers is tough, but thin enough to allow for fine dexterity. www.seattlemarine.net/atlas_gloves

Plastic. You need either used dry cleaning bags, food wrap, or lids to fit over each tray. (Some trays come with a lid, some don't.)

Fertilizer. You want a liquid organic plant food like fish-and-seaweed fertilizer or compost tea bags. Just to be perfectly clear, if the fertilizer is clear, bright green or blue liquid, or "crystals," it's not organic, no matter what the packaging claims.

Spray bottle. With nozzle that mists.

Fan. Small enough to sit on a table and not blow your trays away.

Timer. To turn the lights on and off (optional).

Room. Go where you can control the light coming in from the outside and the temperature stays between 65 and 75 degrees Fahrenheit.

Basic stuff, right? When you have everything together, you are ready to start the seeds. In a bucket or large pot, mix one part compost into three parts of the soil-less mix. The compost gives the little sprouts access to natural nutrients as soon as they grow roots and also helps to keep the mix evenly moist.

Dampen all of the mix. It should feel like a wrung-out sponge, not sopping wet. Pick up a handful and fill the cells in your seedling tray with it. Each cell should be nearly, but not completely full. Press it down, but don't pack it in tight.

When all the cells are full, place two seeds in each of them. Push the seeds in just a bit to be sure they have complete contact with the soil. Sprinkle soil-less mix on top of each cell. Then cover the whole tray with the lid or plastic. Set your trays on a table or the floor. You may want to cover the area with an old sheet or shower curtain to shield it from the dirt and water that inevitably spills as you care for the plants.

The seeds do not need light to germinate, so keep the room dark, if possible. In a day or two, you will see condensation on the plastic, which indicates that the soil-less mix is still moist. Check the tray each day and before the mix dries out completely, pull back the plastic and spritz the soil with water so that it stays constantly damp.

As soon as you see the first sprouts coming up—typically in ten days to two weeks—remove the plastic. Now set up the lights so that you can sit the trays a few inches below them. As the sprouts grow, you want to always keep them no more than two to three inches from the lights. Some growers use the chains that come with the lights attached to a frame, others rest their lights on stacks of bricks or cinder blocks. However you set up your lights, you want to be able to raise them and/or lower the trays to be sure you maintain that two to three inch distance between bulbs and plants.

If you're using a timer, attach it right away. Give the plants light for at least 14 hours each day. You can also leave them on 24 hours a day. Just be sure you are consistent with the amount of light the seedlings get—it has a critical impact on growing productive female plants. Unless you use a timer, your best bet is to keep the lights on all the time.

No, I am not suffering from short-term memory loss caused by smoking too much homegrown organic cannabis. I just can't say enough that you must keep the soil consistently moist so that sprouts have a steady supply of water. At their youngest stages, they can die in less than one dry day. Check them daily and mist the soil whenever it feels dry to the touch.

A tip from Dr. Kindbud: If your seedlings start to look tall and spindly, they are too far from the lights. Move them closer.

First Days

Just about all seeds, including cannabis, contain tiny, round embryonic leaves known as cotyledon (for those of you who like to use the technical terms). A week or two after the seeds sprout, they develop their first set of "true" leaves, the familiar serrated ones you associate with cannabis plants. When they develop their second set of true leaves, you can begin to feed the sprouts. Once a week, add a few drops of the liquid fish-and-seaweed fertilizer or compost tea to the water you spray on the soil.

After the sprouts have two sets of true leaves, set up the fan so that it's two or three feet away from the trays. Run the fan at its lowest speed so that it blows very gently on the sprouts. The light breeze helps the plant develop sturdier stems, so they can better withstand outdoor conditions once they move out. And the breeze also diminishes the risk of fungus forming on top of the constantly moist soil. (If you do see fungus on the soil, sprinkle corn meal or a little more peat on top.) The fan does not need to run all day—you can attach it to the same timer as the lights, if that's convenient for you.

If you planted two seeds in each cell, many of them are likely to have two seedlings in them. In the third or fourth week, pick the seedling in each cell with the thickest stem and most dense leaf cover. Use scissors to snip off the other one. I know, you hate to lose a potential plant, but the remaining one will grow bigger and more productive because it won't be competing for water and nutrients. If you don't do this, you'll have two smaller, weaker plants instead of one healthy one.

In just a few weeks, the seedlings will be more than six inches tall and outgrowing the seedling tray. Your pot plants are ready to be "potted up." You can buy small plastic pots for this or ones formed out of peat and wood pulp, commonly called "Jiffy" pots. Get the four-inch size. Or you can recycle used yogurt cups. Be sure to rinse them out well first and poke a few small holes in the bottom for drainage.

Get together the same mix-and-compost blend you used for starting the seeds, moisten it, and fill each pot about two-thirds full. Now lift up your packs of seedlings and carefully push one out from the bottom. Look at its roots. If they are wrapped around each other tightly, gently work your finger into the middle and spread them apart. Then put it into one of the bigger pots and add soil. Be sure the juncture where the stem meets the roots is at the same level it was in the seedling tray—you don't want it above or below the soil line. Place your fingers on the soil around the stem and gently press to be sure the roots have solid contact with the soil. Repeat this with all the other seedlings.

Remove the plastic cells from the trays, then put the pots in the flat tray bottoms and set them beneath the lights (still just a few inches below the bulbs). You can now begin watering them simply by adding it to the tray. They will grow roots down through the soil to absorb it. Once a week, let the tray dry out and give each plant a dose of the liquid fish fertilizer or compost tea diluted (though not as much as before) in water. Keep using the fan and watch how thick and healthy the stems grow.

The Organic Guide To Growing High-Quality Cannabis

Moving Out

The time to move your seedlings outside is the same as if you were planting seeds. That is, as soon as possible after your last frost date. About two weeks before that, begin preparing your seedlings for their life outside by the process called "hardening off." Take the plants outside and put them in a sheltered location—out of direct sun and wind—for a few hours, then bring them back indoors and put under the lights again. Over the next two weeks, gradually increase the amount of time the plants have outside and how much direct sunlight they get. Be sure the soil stays damp—sunlight and wind dry out the soil a lot faster than fluorescent lights and you want the plants to keep growing stronger during the hardening off period.

Late afternoon on an overcast day is ideal for transplanting. This gives the plant time to adjust to the new conditions before facing the hot sun. The steps to transplanting outside are not much different than those you followed when potting up your seedlings.

1. Open a hole. The planting hole should be as deep and slightly bigger in diameter than the plant's container.

2. Water before planting. Until the roots start growing, they can't draw water from the soil. So make sure they are well-hydrated before taking them out of their pots.

3. Tip the plant from the pot. Spread your hand on top of the pot, with your fingers around the plant's stem. Turn the pot upside down and gently squeeze it or push the plant out from the bottom with your other hand. If you must tug it out, pull it by its leaves rather than the stem (if a leaf comes off, no harm done; damage the stem and the plant will not survive).

4. Loosen the roots. Look at the roots and if they have wrapped around and around the plant, gently pull a few loose with your fingers. This helps them grow out into the surrounding soil instead of continuing to encircle each other.

5. Set it into the hole. Put the seedling in the hole at the same depth it was in its pot, so that the spot where the stem meets the roots is level with the ground.

6. Backfill and water again. Push the soil you removed when digging back into the hole and press gently to ensure that the roots have solid contact with the soil. Keep the soil consistently moist until you see the plant start to grow new leaves.

For the first 24 hours or so after you transplant, the stems and leaves may appear a bit droopy. This is a normal symptom of "transplant shock" and they should recover in a day or two. If a plant doesn't straighten up and look adapted after a of couple days, firm the soil around the stem with your hands to make sure it has solid contact with the roots.

QUICK HITS

- Test seeds for viability by floating them before planting.
- Start them indoors if you can in "soil-less" mix.
- Plant seeds outside or move seedlings out after the last frost date in spring.
- Keep seeds and young plants constantly moist.

CHAPTER SIX

Males, Females, Long Days and Dark Nights

Growing cannabis plants is easy. But I'm going to assume you want to do more than just grow a big, leafy, fragrant pot plant. You want to harvest a bumper crop of all-natural, plump buds loaded with THC, right? To do that, you need to know a bit about the plant, its life cycle, and reproductive process. Yes, we're now going to talk about sex and plants.

Sex Talk

In its natural state, cannabis is an "annual" plant, as opposed to a "perennial" such as trees, shrubs, and tulips. Annuals germinate, grow their roots, stems, and leaves, mature, reproduce, and die in a single season. New plants grow from seeds. Cannabis is what scientists call "dioecious," meaning there are male and female plants. (Some hybrid varieties also tend to produce hermaphrodites, which have both male and female reproductive parts on the same plant.) Under normal conditions, a batch of cannabis seeds produces a roughly equal number of males and females. Seeds result when male plants pollinate female plants. After the females

are pollinated, they form the clusters of flowers that you know as buds. If the females are not pollinated, they still produce buds but they will be seedless. Marijuana that has no seeds is known as "sinsemilla" (pronounced "sense-ah-me-ya") and for many growers seedless buds are the goal.

The reproductive organs that develop as the plants mature are known as stamens on the males and pistils on the female. Both start as tiny nubs that form between the branches. When I say tiny, I mean they are about the size of the tip on a ballpoint pen. They are slightly different in appearance, and learning to identify them accurately will help you harvest lots of buds.

Males produce pollen and then they shed it, or release it into the air. At or about the same time, the female's ovaries open and extend a tube that captures the pollen. Those tubes are the "hairs" that you see when you look closely at a bud. The microscopic grains of pollen attach themselves to the tube and then travel up to the ovaries. The pollen has half of the chromosomes of a mature plant and the ovary provides the complementary other half of the chromosomes. When the two sets of chromosomes link up, you have reproduction. Sounds a lot like what you learned in eighth grade about human reproduction, doesn't it?

The life cycle of cannabis naturally takes about four to six months to complete, depending on the strain you are growing and the conditions in which it's grown. With care and attention, you can manage the reproductive process, but bear in mind that the plant has evolved and adapted over thousands of years to grow in ways that ensure its survival for a few more millennia. You will harvest the best-tasting, most potent, purest, and kindest buds if you work with, rather than against, its natural tendencies.

Girls Only

Left alone, male cannabis plants will fertilize most, if not all, of the females. That's what they are for. If that happens, the buds you get will be predominantly seeds with little of the unfertilized flowers that are the smokeable content. If you isolate all the females, they will produce seed-free buds. Just what you want for this year's harvest, but you won't have any seeds to start the next season's crop. Leaving a few females to be pollinated can give you the best of both options.

You want to learn to separate the boys from the girls. The two types of plants have some immediately visible differences. Female plants typically are shorter and have more branches than males do. Also, the females are generally leafier, especially at the top, while you see more stem and fewer leaves on the males, particularly on the lateral limbs.

These are helpful early signs, but they're not conclusive enough to trust. You want to identify the reproductive organs. They appear along the plant's main stem at intersections where lateral branches connect to the stem. Botanists call these spots "nodes." At first, the two types of reproductive organs look very similar. But within a day or even hours you will notice differences.

Male organs develop a curved, claw shape, and then change into rounded balls hanging down from very thin filaments. The balls have five segments, or petals, which separate slightly at the top. They can be yellow or whitish, or fully green.

The females develop long white, yellow, or pink "hairs," the pistils, sticking out from a thin, fluted membrane called the "sheath." The pistils typically show up in pairs. Those hairs are covered with resin to help the pollen attach to them.

After pollination, the males die quickly. The females live up to five months longer if they are only lightly pollinated or not at all.

Reproductive Care

Males growing outdoors begin showing their organs approximately three weeks before the females. Exactly when depends on your climate, whether you started with seeds or transplants, and the strain. At northern latitudes males may first appear as early as

mid-July. Strains adapted to growing in the South may start revealing the males as late as the middle of September.

Pollination can occur within days or even hours after the reproductive organs appear, so you want to be aware when this time approaches and check your plants as often as possible. As soon as you see a male plant in an outdoor plot, cut it off at its base. Try to shake it as little as possible so that it doesn't shed its pollen near any female.

If you are able to grow without fear of discovery, you can protect your females with a technique that farmers and gardeners use to protect tomatoes, corn, and other plants from unwanted cross-pollination. When you positively identify a female plant, cover it with horticultural fabric (widely sold under the brand name Reemay). It lets light, air, and water get through, but pollen won't. Cut the sheet of fabric into pieces roughly the size of your plants' leaf canopy. Drape the fabric over the plant and tie it loosely with twine. You can remove the cover when you're certain you've removed all the males.

Growers who start their seeds indoors—either for planting outside or in—have even more control over the development of males and females. In the seed-starting section of this book, you'll see that I recommended giving the plants at least 14 hours of light each day. When your plants are about four inches tall with a few sets of leaves, reduce the light to just eight hours a day. In a few days to a week, the males will reveal themselves. After you've culled them all out, go back to giving your females 14 hours of light a day.

See the Light

That trick of changing the light pattern to get the males to reveal themselves tells you that light plays a critical role in cannabis's reproductive process. Throughout their lives, the plants contain a hormone that is turned off by even low levels of light. When the dark periods last long enough for the hormone level to reach

critical mass, the reproductive cycle is triggered. The plant redirects its energy from growing more limbs and leaves to flowering.

With the knowledge of how the balance of light vs. dark—or "photoperiod"—affects your cannabis's reproductive process, you can influence the timing of when your harvest comes in, critical for growing outdoors in a short-season climate. Growers everywhere can manipulate the photoperiod to increase the quality and quantity of buds they harvest—all without relying on chemical fertilizers.

Northern Nights

The further away from the Equator that you move, the greater the difference between daylight and nighttime hours in summer. At the Equator, the longest day of the year (the summer solstice) is about 12.5 hours. In Maine, that day lasts about 16 hours.

In natural conditions, male and female cannabis plants flower after about two weeks of nights that last more than ten hours. In the northern U.S. and Canada, as well as at high elevations further south, frost may strike the plants before the nights are long enough to trigger flowering. In these conditions, you might think you have to settle for indoor growing or give up growing altogether. But not to worry—by making the nights artificially longer, you can set the budding process in motion when you want.

In early to mid-August—earlier the further north you live—start covering your plants for part of each day to block the light. You want to do this while the weather is still mild enough for the plants to continue growing for another month after flowering. Your goal is to extend the nights by a couple hours, so that your plants are in the dark for about 13 hours. You can cover them with anything opaque, like a tarp, black plastic mulch, or two to three layers of plastic trash bags. Also, be aware of and work with the natural conditions. For example, if the plants are shaded in the morning,

cover them each evening for a couple hours before the sun goes down and uncover them around eight a.m. each morning.

Any light that reaches the plants—from streetlights, car headlights, head lamps, and even flashlights—can disrupt the long-night cycle you are working on. Take extra care to be sure no light gets to your plants while they are cloaked. If you are growing your crop in containers, you can simply move the pots to a dark location. Again, be sure during the dark cycle that no light gets to the plants from a window or even a crack in the door.

Older, more developed plants respond quicker to the changing light-dark pattern than young plants do. A six-month old plant may start to flower after just four days of extended nights, while a plant that's just six weeks old can take more than two weeks of long nights before flowering. For this reason, among several others I've explained in previous chapters, if you are growing outdoors in a cool climate you benefit greatly by starting your plants indoors and then transplanting them outside. The more mature they are earlier in the season, the better your harvest of buds will be.

Bulking Up Your Plants

Now you understand how to get your plants to start flowering. But say you want the opposite, to inhibit your plants from flowering. Why would you want to do that? To give the plants time to grow bigger and put on more limbs (on which more flowers will form) before they start to reproduce. In warm climates, this can dramatically increase the amount of buds you harvest—by as much as double for each extra month of growth the plant does before flowering.

You're probably already guessing how to prevent the plant from flowering—by interrupting the dark period with light. You can do this with artificial lights. You can use electric lights, car headlights, or an industrial-strength flashlight. The most reliable way to do this is to put up a string of lights attached to a timer.

No matter which light you use, be sure it shines on the entire plant. Any limbs kept in a shadow may start to bloom and spoil your effort to delay flowering. It doesn't take much light. On a clear night, the full moon emits about .01 foot-candles. Just .03 foot-candles is bright enough to do the job. The lights need to be on only for a few minutes to work. The ideal time is between midnight and three a.m., so that you break up the longest period of darkness.

When your plants are big and you are ready for them to flower, shield them from exposure to any light for at least ten hours each day. In just a few days, they'll start their reproductive process and you can start looking forward to your harvest of big buds.

QUICK HITS

• Cannabis plants can be male or female. The buds are clusters of flowers on the females. If they are pollinated by the males, you get seeds.
• Shortening daylight hours triggers the reproductive process.
• Managing the light and dark cycles allows you to speed up or slow it down the reproductive process.
• The bigger and more mature the plant is when it starts to reproduce, the more buds you'll get and more potency they will have.

10 Useful Books

Organic Gardening: *A Practical Guide to Natural Gardens, From Planning and Planting to Harvesting and Maintenance* by Christine Lavelle. Southwater Press. 256 pages.

An essential reference guide to natural gardening, showing how to apply organic principals to all aspects of garden planning, design, and maintenance.

Rodale's Ultimate Encyclopedia of Organic Gardening: *The Indispensable Green Resource for Every Gardener* by Fern Marshall Bradley. Rodale Books. 720 pages.

A go-to resource for decades, this book has everything you could need to know to create non-toxic gardens in any part of the country.

The New Organic Grower: *A Master's Manual of Tools and Techniques for the Home and Market Gardener* by Elliot Coleman. Chelsea Green Publishing. 340 pages.

Master grower Coleman presents a simple, effective formula for growing quality organic vegetables.

The Organic Gardener's Handbook of Natural Insect and Disease Control: *A Complete Problem-Solving Guide to Keeping Your Garden and Yard Healthy Without Chemicals* by Barbara Ellis. Rodale Books. 544 pages.

The title pretty much says it all.

Garden Insects of North America: *The Ultimate Guide to Backyard Bugs* by Whitney Cranshaw. Princeton University Press. 672 pages.

The title says it's the "ultimate guide" and it really is.

Teeming with Microbes: *A Gardener's Guide to the Soil Food Web* by Jeff Lowenfels. Timber Press. 196 pages.

A must-read for any gardener looking to create a sustainable, healthy garden without chemicals.

The Soul of Soil: *A Soil-Building Guide for Master Gardeners and Farmers* by Grace Gershuny. Chelsea Green Publishing. 192 pages.

This book provides essential information for those attempting to grow organically.

Let It Rot: *The Gardener's Guide to Composting* by Stu Campbell. Storey Publishing. 153 pages.

Horticulture Review called this book, "the composter's bible."

Worms Eat My Garbage: *How to Set Up and Maintain a Worm Composting System* by Mary Appelhof. Flower Press. 162 pages

The definitive guide to vermicomposting.

The Book of Weeds: How to Deal With Plants that Behave Badly by Kenneth Thompson. DK Publishing. 192 pages.

How to recognize, control, and eliminate weeds.

All Leaves, All The Time

Growing for maximum buds is kind of a boom-and-bust cycle. You grow the plants for months, waiting to enjoy the fruits of your labor. Then the harvest comes in all at once and you wait until the next season to start growing again.

Some growers, though, prefer a constant supply of leaves to a big haul of buds. Leaves are less potent than buds, but still can be effective and are often enjoyed in a mix with tobacco. If you want to harvest a constant supply of shoots and leaves, get your plants more than 18 hours of light every day. They will continue growing and may eventually flower but will not pollinate or form buds. They may lose their vigor as they age, so be prepared to replace them.

A tip from Dr. Kindbud: The reproductive parts of male and female plants are very small and may look alike at first. Check them out with a magnifying lens to be sure you get a positive identification.

CHAPTER SEVEN

Water Wise

I f you've been paying attention so far (you have been, right?), you now know that when your plants are just starting out, they must have constant moisture to survive. You need to check them daily and sprinkle them whenever the top few inches of soil dry out. As your plants mature, they still require constant, even moisture but how you provide it changes.

Outdoor Watering

For the first few days after you transplant, keep watering the seedlings just as you did indoors. That is, daily sprinkling to keep the soil around the roots damp at all times. But once you see the seedlings starting to grow again, you want to encourage them to build a deep and wide root system that can hold up a tall, bushy plant and scavenge in the soil for water and nutrients throughout the season. You accomplish this by watering less frequently but more heavily.

About two weeks after you have transplanted your crop outdoors, cut back on the daily watering. Instead, push your index finger

two knuckles deep into the surrounding soil whenever you check on your plants. Feel damp? If so, don't water the plants, no matter what they look like. They may appear to be wilting in high heat, but that does not mean they are dehydrated. Plants curl their leaves in the heat to slow down transpiration, or the loss of water from the leaves.

When the soil is definitely dry, give each plant a gallon of water. Pour it on slowly so that it can percolate down deep into the soil, rather than running off your plot and leaving only the top few inches wet.

Water your plants directly on the soil. They can absorb very little moisture through their leaves, so watering leaves, even when they look wilted, is wasteful and doesn't help the plant build a large root system. Pour the water in an area up to a foot away from the stem in all directions. Again, this entices the roots to grow wide rather than just below the stem.

You can use a watering can or a hose to water your plants. If the hose has a spray nozzle, put it on the shower setting, not jet (you don't want to blow the plants out of the soil, do you?). Even more efficient is a "soaker" hose, which is made of water-permeable material that lets moisture slowly "weep" out into the soil. (You'll find them in hardware stores, garden centers, and online.)

Drip, Drip, Drip

For maximum efficiency and reliability, many small-scale farmers and home gardeners set up drip irrigation systems. They comprise a network of tubes through which the water flows to emitters set at intervals chosen by the grower. The emitters deliver water right to the plants' roots and nowhere else. And by attaching the system to a timer, you can be sure the plants get exactly the right amount of water, exactly when they need it, so you don't have to find the time to do it each day.

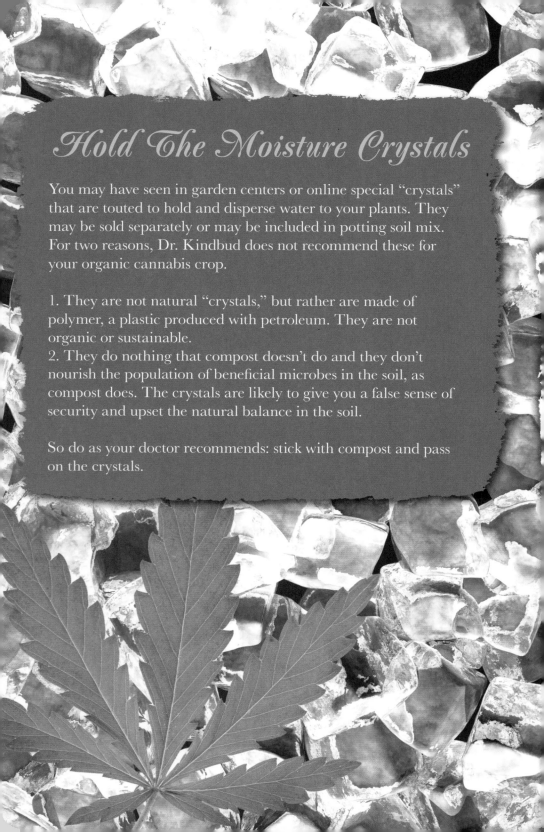

Hold The Moisture Crystals

You may have seen in garden centers or online special "crystals" that are touted to hold and disperse water to your plants. They may be sold separately or may be included in potting soil mix. For two reasons, Dr. Kindbud does not recommend these for your organic cannabis crop.

1. They are not natural "crystals," but rather are made of polymer, a plastic produced with petroleum. They are not organic or sustainable.
2. They do nothing that compost doesn't do and they don't nourish the population of beneficial microbes in the soil, as compost does. The crystals are likely to give you a false sense of security and upset the natural balance in the soil.

So do as your doctor recommends: stick with compost and pass on the crystals.

Timing does matter. The ideal time to water your plants is first thing in the morning. This gives them time to absorb the moisture and get it out to the leaves and buds before the sun evaporates it during the heat of the day. The next best time to water is in the evening, an hour or so before dusk. It is especially critical to direct water to the ground when you're watering at the end of the day. Moisture left on the leaves overnight can become a host to fungal diseases that can kill your crop or at least ruin its flavor. (You've probably tasted musty buds at one time or another. They likely had mold, mildew, or other fungus on them either while they were growing or in storage.)

Mulch and then Mulch Again

I can't emphasize enough the importance of keeping a layer of mulch on top of the soil at all times. Mulch is absolutely vital for keeping your crop evenly hydrated. This works in two different ways. First, by shielding the soil from the sun, moisture evaporates from it more slowly than if it were exposed to the bright light.

Second, mulch keeps weed seeds in the soil from getting enough light to germinate. (There always are weed seeds in the soil; they blow in from surrounding areas and birds, squirrels, and other critters deposit them there.) Weeds—those plants you are not trying to grow—are not just unsightly; they are thieves. They siphon water and nutrients away from your crop. Also, weeds often are hosts to pests and diseases that can move over to your crop. So, once more, keep a consistent three-inch (or more) layer of grass clippings, straw, shredded leaves, or pine needles on every bit of your plot at all times. Replenish the layer throughout the growing season as it breaks down, decomposes, and nourishes the beneficial microbes in the soil.

The Organic Guide To Growing High-Quality Cannabis

Indoor Irrigation

If you're growing your crop inside, the watering plan is different. Because the roots have limited room to spread out, you must keep them constantly moist. But you must also beware not to overwater them—plants' roots need oxygen and can drown in saturated soil. Watering indoor plants properly requires balancing both of these concerns.

First, use the biggest container to hold your plants that you can. If you're using standard plastic nursery pots (sold by nursery wholesalers and online), get the five gallon-size, and if you have room the ten gallon is even better. The bigger the container, the bigger the root system, the more water and nutrients it can take up, the bigger and more productive your plants will be.

If you don't use standard nursery pots, be sure that any container you use has drainage holes in the bottom. You may have grown other plants in containers—or heard from people who do—and believe that you should put gravel, Styrofoam peanuts, or other loose material at the bottom of the container to enhance the drainage. Don't do it. Reducing the volume of soil in the pot decreases the roots' mass and that limits the size and vigor of your plant. Smaller plants and fewer roots leads to a reduced harvest.

The other key to keeping your plants from becoming oversaturated is the soil mix. Never use soil you dug up outside for growing indoors—it is too dense and holds too much water. Packaged potting mixes are okay, but to keep your crop organic pass on bags with fertilizer included. The fertilizers are almost always the synthetic kind. The best soil mix for keeping your plants consistently hydrated is a blend of three parts peat moss with two parts compost and one part perlite or vermiculite. (This is more compost than the mix I recommended using for starting seeds.) The peat ensures that the mix drains well, the compost provides essential nutrients and moderate moisture retention. Perlite and vermiculite also absorb water and then gradually release it back into the soil.

The ideal time to water your plants outdoors is first thing in the morning so they have it available during the day. Likewise, the best time to water indoor plants is at the start of their daily light cycle. Wet soil in dark conditions is prone to fungal growth.

If your water comes from a reservoir or other municipal source rather than a well, there's a very good chance it has been treated with chlorine to kill bacteria and neutralize impurities. Chlorine is an acid and continually pouring chlorinated water on your plants can lower the soil's pH. Fortunately, chlorine is fairly volatile—just by leaving the water sitting in an open container before you use it for a day or even a few hours, most if not all of the chlorine evaporates. Don't take water straight from your tap to your plants; first let it dechlorinate.

You can use a small watering can or pitcher to water your indoor plants. Or you can set up a "drip irrigation" system like many greenhouse operators depend on. These systems put water straight on plants' roots, deliver just the right amount, and can be attached to a timer so that your plants get water on the same schedule no matter what you are up to. A basic set-up costs about $50 to $60—not much for the confidence that your plants are consistently watered. More elaborate kits cost up to $300, with features that make using them even easier for you.

QUICK HITS

- After transplants start growing outside, give them a deep soaking once or twice a week when the soil is dry.
- Pour water directly on the soil, not the leaves.
- Water early in the day outdoors or at the start of the light cycle indoors.
- Never use outdoor soil for indoor plants.
- Dechlorinate water by letting it sit before using it.

Save the Rain

The water that comes out of your tap is probably nice and clear. If it's from a municipal supply rather than a well, chances are the water has been treated with a variety of chemicals, particularly chlorine and, in many areas, fluoride. Most of the chlorine dissipates if you let the water sit in an open container for a day or so before using it.

But the purest and most natural supply of water for your organic cannabis crop is rainwater. Of course, you can't turn it on and off whenever you need it. But you can save rain when it falls and use it to water your crop when you need to. A simple rain barrel, which you can make or buy, attaches to your home's gutters and stores the water in a covered (to keep mosquitoes from breeding in it) container.

Saving rain is not only good for your plants. When you save rainwater, you reduce your ecological footprint by diminishing your demand for water that must be purified and pumped to your spigot. Rainwater makes your crop purer and more organic. That's always a good vibe, isn't it?

A tip from Dr. Kindbud: If you're using a watering can or a bucket, pour water slowly onto the soil rather than dumping it all at once. You want it to seep down deep into the soil, not disperse near the surface.

CHAPTER EIGHT

Feeding Time

Y ou've read this before, but I have to say it again here. The key to growing a productive, high-quality organic cannabis crop is by building healthy, biologically-active soil. You do that by continually replenishing the organic matter in the soil. The most beneficial organic matter is compost, because it is ready for the microbes in the soil to convert into nutrients in the form plants use them.

No matter what you've heard or read elsewhere, there's no shortcut to get around building healthy soil. No "miracle" product or fertilizer can circumvent the need for it. You feed the microbes and they nourish your plants with the healthy, well-rounded diet they evolved with.

In contrast, synthetic fertilizers are to plants what anabolic steroids are to people. They are quickly absorbed and can stimulate astounding growth in a short period of time. But they are addicting—you have to continue using them to maintain the growth—and eventually the plant (or person) becomes weaker and often dies prematurely because it is not able to sustain the extraordinary growth. Synthetic fertilizers are not balanced with all the macro and micronutrients in the proportions plants need them. Most synthetic fertilizers are high in salts, so persistent use raises the salt content of your soil and dehydrates the beneficial microbe population you are nurturing. Chemical fertilizer formulas now rely on phosphoric acid to raise the phosphorous content quickly and cheaply. Some research has found that phosphoric acid neutralizes other important trace minerals in the soil.

The environment suffers when you use synthetic fertilizers, too. They are typically made with petroleum, and we all know the ecological (as well as geopolitical) impact of extracting, refining, and distributing oil. Even more immediate, synthetic fertilizers are not absorbed by plants right away, so much of it washes into underground water and flows into rivers, lakes, and ponds. This leads to excessive algae growth that is choking many fresh bodies of water and the aquatic life they support.

If none of those reasons are compelling enough to pass on the synthetic fertilizer, think about the quality of your buds. The ammonia taste that too often overpowers the fresh natural flavors of high-quality pot is the result of using synthetic fertilizers. To get the best-tasting and highest quality, stick with organic fertilizers.

Label Savvy

How can you tell if a fertilizer is synthetic or organic? First, look at the package label. If you see that the product is "OMRI-approved," you can be certain it is organic. OMRI stands for Organic Materials Review Institute, which is the organization designated by the U.S. Department of Agriculture to determine if a fertilizer or other farming product is acceptable for certified organic production. Lots of fertilizer products have the OMRI label—you can learn more about this at omri.org.

But the lack of an OMRI label does not mean the fertilizer is definitely not organic. Look at the product's ingredient list. Synthetic fertilizers typically contain ammonium nitrate or urea (which is a manufactured copy of nitrogen-rich animal urine—I kid you not). The main ingredients in organic fertilizers are recognizable, though admittedly not exactly appetizing either.

When you look at fertilizer packages, you see a ratio listed on the label. The ratio is always a three number set, like 10-5-10. This refers to the proportions of nitrogen, phosphorus, and potassium, or N-P-K, in the fertilizer. All packaged plant foods must list their N-P-K ratings on their labels. All are essential macronutrients plants need to survive. Briefly, nitrogen feeds leaf and stem growth, phosphorus supports root and flower development, and potassium (also known as potash) aids the plant in processing the other two. The N-P-K ratings of organic fertilizers tend to be lower than synthetics, but the balance is the most significant piece of information. Nitrogen-rich fertilizers are most valuable early in the growing season, to help the plant build a sturdy stem and dense leaf cover. As the plant matures, you want to give it less nitrogen and more phosphorus to stimulate flower (that is, bud) production.

Free Food

The most valuable organic fertilizers don't have labels and are not sold in stores. You can't feed your plants better than with a steady diet of well-balanced homemade compost. But if you can't make

Feeding Time 🍁

enough compost for your needs, you can score free fertilizer from a variety of local sources.

The classic organic fertilizer is manure from barnyard animals. If you live near a farm where cows, sheep, goats, chickens, or horses are raised, you can often get manure for free if you'll shovel or haul it. (A trash can or other container with a lid comes in handy for transporting the stuff in your car.) Take the "stable bedding," too, which is the straw, wood chips, or other stuff on the ground. It adds healthy amounts of organic matter to your soil along with the nutrient-rich manure.

You can also use the waste from pet rabbits, guinea pigs, and other herbivorous (non-meat eating) animals. Rabbits' waste pellets are like little fertilizer pills, which gradually release their valuable nutrients. They are so nutritious and devoid of contaminant risk that you can just scatter them around the garden before planting and work them into the soil. Plus, leftover alfalfa rabbit food is not just for the bunnies—it nourishes plants, too. It contains a natural fatty-acid growth stimulant, trianconatol, along with a balanced supply of N-P-K.

Do you have a fish tank? Save the dirty water because all the fish poop in it is nutrient-rich food for your plants. And if you happen to be at a zoo or circus, you can take home the droppings of their herbivores to use as fertilizer.

When using manure, remember this important caution: If it is fresh, do not apply it directly to your garden during the growing season. It can be very "hot"—or decomposing very rapidly—and can literally burn your plants. Spread it on your plot early in spring, about sixty days before you plan to plant. If you get a load (sorry) during the growing season, add it to your compost pile or let it sit and decompose for about two months before spreading it on your plot. Exceptions: The fish tank water can be applied immediately, but if it is very dirty, dilute it in an equal amount of

clean water before using it on your plants. Rabbit dung can also be applied to your plot without waiting for it to compost.

Local industry can be another valuable source of free organic fertilizers. Cottonseed hulls and alfalfa, fish waste from a cannery, and used grains from your nearby brewery are all examples of raw materials that will be discarded by manufacturers but will be a source of nutrients for your soil. Poultry processing facilities accumulate hundreds of pounds of feather waste every day. Much of it is sold to produce supplements for livestock, but it's worth asking for some because feathers are a source of very slow-release nitrogen. About four months before the growing season, mix into your soil as much as 5 pounds of feather meal per 100 square feet. Live near a cement producer? Ask there for kiln dust, a by-product that can supply potassium to your plants. (Just be sure to inquire about whether the factory fires industrial waste rather than raw ingredients to make cement. You don't want kiln dust from industrial waste.)

You may be throwing away fertilizer in your own kitchen. The leftovers from your daily cup of joe give your plants a well-rounded jolt of nitrogen, phosphorus, potassium, and various trace minerals. Ask for the grounds at your local coffee shop if you want more—Starbucks has a "Grounds for Gardeners" campaign to keep them out of landfills. Coffee grounds are highly acidic, so if your soil tends to be low pH or if you have tons of the grounds, put them in a compost pile first rather than directly on the soil.

Chicken eggshells are 93 percent calcium carbonate, making them a rich source of the essential mineral, calcium, and are an effective alternative to purchasing lime to help raise the pH of your soil. Dry your eggshells in a pan in the oven with either the pilot light or at the lowest temperature setting. Crumble them by hand and pulverize them in a blender or food processor, then sprinkle over acidic soil. Ground clam and oyster shells serve the same purpose, as well as many other shells you can find on the beach.

A tip from Dr. Kindbud: Beware of bagged fertilizers containing "biosolids," which is an industry term for sewage sludge. It's nasty stuff that often contains heavy metals which can disrupt the chemistry of your soil.

Beaches offer you another trove of free fertilizer. Seaweed, particularly kelp, is loaded with potassium (approximately 20-25 percent). If you live near or often visit the beach, gather kelp and store it in a large drum or plastic trash barrel filled with water. Cover and allow it to decompose for two months. You will be left with a concentrated solution, which you can dilute with water to make a spray you can use to fertilize your plants.

Growers living near mushroom farms can often ask for the "spent" compost that is discarded after each crop. It's high in both organic matter and phosphorus. Researchers have found that it turbocharges the yields of organic vegetable beds.

Burn wood in a fireplace or stove? The ash contains 2 percent phosphate and 6 percent potash, along with a rich supply of calcium. Wood ash also adds magnesium, iron, and aluminum, among other trace minerals, to your soil. Hardwoods tend to contain greater amounts of nutrients. Bear in mind, though, that wood ash is highly alkaline—often with a pH around 11—so use it sparingly. Don't use wood ashes in garden beds where the soil pH is already optimal. Instead, add them to your compost pile.

I want to mention one more easy-to-get, free source of fertilizer for your plot. Your liquid waste. That's right, human urine is 46 percent nitrogen and has higher concentrations of nitrogen, phosphorus, and potassium than most commercial fertilizers. Not only that, but these elements are in an extremely soluble and available form, which makes urine a great starter fertilizer. Don't go outside and pee on your pot patch—it needs to be diluted before you apply it to your plants. Mix it with ten parts water and distribute evenly.

Slang Names for Marijuana

Bud
Buddha
Cheeba
Chronic
Dank
Doobage
Dope
Ganja
Grass
Green
Herb
Hippie Lettuce
Hoobastank
Kind
Kush

Loco weed
Maryjane
Mother Nature
Nug
Oregano
Pot
Puff
Reefer
Skizzunk
Skunk
Shit
Smoke
Spliff
Tea
Weed

Fast Foods

All of the free, natural fertilizers, especially compost, feed the
beneficial microbes in the soil, which ultimately creates the
ideal soil for your organic cannabis crop. Add them continually,
year after year, and you will nourish your plants in ways that no
packaged product can. But when you're just starting out or where
you don't have access to your own natural ingredients, you can buy
fertilizers in bags and bottles that give your plants the boost they
need without turning your organic buds into "chem" schwag.

True organic fertilizers are always "slow-release," because they
nourish plants as they gradually break down. When you look at the
ingredients, they should be familiar words rather than chemical
compounds. Feathermeal, cottonseed meal, or alfalfa meal are
common main ingredients. You will also find chicken manure
(pressed into pellets) and one brand that is made from insect
excrement and sold as Kricket Krap.

Granulated fertilizers like these are easy to apply to a large plot.
They do need time to break down and begin feeding your plants,
so mix the amount recommended on the package into your soil
about thirty days before planting. Don't believe that piling on
excessive amounts of fertilizer makes your plants bigger, stronger,
and more productive. The extra nutrients may cause you to grow
a super-huge plant that doesn't yield a lot of high-quality buds. A
steady, balanced supply of nutrients is the key to maximizing the
potential of your plants.

Seedlings, new transplants, and plants growing in containers need
a faster, more direct delivery of nutrients. Liquid fertilizers handle
the job. But stay away from any that are bright green or blue, or
that smell like they're better suited to cleaning your toilet than
feeding your all-natural buds. Instead, look for formulas with fish
and seaweed as their primary ingredients. Most garden centers
carry them these days—Neptune's Harvest and Alaska are two
widely-distributed brands. Experienced organic gardeners also rely

The Organic Guide To Growing High-Quality Cannabis

on compost tea, which you can make or buy. It is full of nutrients and those beneficial microbes that help feed and keep your plants healthy.

Liquid fertilizers may come in a bottle full of a concentrate or as a powder you mix with water. Either way, start by giving your plants a small amount of nutrients diluted in water. As the plants grow, you can increase the concentration. Just keep reminding yourself that when it comes to fertilizer, even organic ones, more is not better.

Seedlings can use a weekly feeding with a very low concentration of fertilizer. Give your outside plants their first feeding about two weeks after you transplant them outdoors, and then about every two weeks after that. If you can't get to them every other week, the most critical times to feed them are two weeks after you transplant them outdoors, and then at least twice more at two-week intervals. Once the plants stop growing taller and begin their reproductive process, stop feeding them. You want them to direct their energy into bud formation, not growing a bigger plant.

QUICK HITS

- Feed the soil before the plant.
- Pick up free organic fertilizers from nearby farms, food processors and coastal areas.
- When buying bagged fertilizer, look for slow-release formulas and be sure you recognize the ingredients.
- Feed every other week until flowering commences.

Worm's Do

The most nutritious and quickly absorbed organic fertilizer you can give your plants comes from worms. Technically referred to as "vermicompost" or worm "castings," the semi-liquid stuff that worms excrete is the best food for seedlings and plants growing in containers. You can buy it (*there's* a business opportunity you probably haven't thought of) or you can get a worm bin in your house, feed them your kitchen scraps, and collect the castings for your plants. You need a lot of worms and vegetable scraps to produce enough castings for an outdoor crop, but you can collect plenty for container plants or to blend with your soil mix when you're starting seeds.

Worm compost tends to be kind of costly, and is often sold in little boutique bags. If you want to make your own, it's easy and fun. You can buy a kit at composters.com or from many other sources. You can also just get worms—red wrigglers are the best species—and a plastic type storage bin (like Rubbermaid makes), add shredded newspaper for bedding and fruit and vegetable waste (carrot peels, apple cores, etc) from your kitchen, and then let the worms do their stuff. For complete instructions on how to set up, maintain, and extract the castings from your worm bin, go to wormwoman.com.

CHAPTER NINE

Bad Weeds vs. Good Weed

Weeds are thieves. I'm not talking about the good stuff you're trying to grow. When I say "weeds," I mean the plants that move in whenever and wherever you turn the soil. You've heard the phrase, "Nature hates a vacuum"? It is surely true about bare soil. Weeds are the opportunistic plants that have evolved to fill any space on the ground where other plants aren't growing. Many of them are attractive and in some settings they may even be beneficial, but you don't want them in your cannabis plot. They siphon water and nutrients away from your plants and can harbor pests and diseases you don't want anywhere near your crop.

Too many farmers, gardeners, landscapers, and homeowners go for the nuclear option to eliminate weeds: herbicides. They are powerful chemicals that kill weeds when you spray or spread them on your soil. Herbicides are known to leach into groundwater and harm wildlife. They have also been linked to increased cancer risk in dogs that are exposed to them. And they may get into your organic pot plants and spoil all the hard work you've put into keeping them pure. Passing on the toxic herbicides does not mean that you need to let

weeds invade your plot. There are organic strategies that you can trust to help ward off plant invaders from your pot patch.

Mulch. I've said it before (and chances are, I'll say it again) keep your soil covered at all times with a layer of organic mulch. This prevents light from reaching weed seeds and sprouts, helping reduce the amount that germinate and end up being a nuisance. The few weeds that do poke through the layer of mulch usually are shallowly rooted and easy to pull.

Spread a thick layer (three or more inches deep) of straw, grass clippings, shredded leaves, or bark chips on your plot right after planting. Organic mulch like these wash away and/or decompose over time, so replenish the layer periodically throughout the growing season. Bonus: these mulches are organic matter that nourishes your soil as it decomposes.

For even better weed protection, first cover the soil with a layer of newspaper (the black-and-white pages only), kraft paper (the paper used to make grocery bags), or cardboard. They are nearly impenetrable. Cover them with a layer of the grass, leaves, straw, or bark to keep them from blowing away.

Weed barriers. A more expensive but very effective tool is a weed-blocking fabric. If you've ever worked in landscaping, you're probably familiar with this. It is a manufactured blanket of tightly woven fibers that allow air and water through, but not light. You spread it on the soil and then make small slits in the fabric where you want to put your plants. While weed barriers work very well, they have two distinct drawbacks. First, they are very conspicuous, so they'll draw attention to your patch, while the colors and textures of the organic mulches appear much more natural. Secondly, they don't nourish the soil life as organic mulches do. If you use a weed barrier, you have to make a conscious effort to replenish the essential organic matter in the soil when the barrier is off during the dormant season.

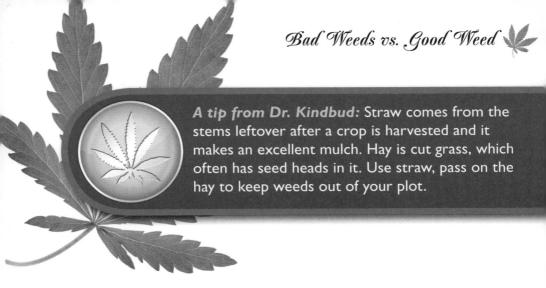

A tip from Dr. Kindbud: Straw comes from the stems leftover after a crop is harvested and it makes an excellent mulch. Hay is cut grass, which often has seed heads in it. Use straw, pass on the hay to keep weeds out of your plot.

Handpulling. I'm not going to sugar-coat the obvious: pulling weeds by hand is tedious and can be hard on your back and knees. But I've found that pulling weeds when you have a good buzz on can be very relaxing. And in a small space like a little plot of pot, you can make it easier by just keeping up with it. That is, pull out the biggest weeds whenever you check on the patch and then you won't find yourself with a big mess to clean up all at once. Remember that you need to yank out the roots or the weed is very likely to just grow back, probably bigger and stronger. Moisten the soil around the roots, if it's not already, and then grasp the weed's stem as close to the ground as possible when you pull. Also, always pull weeds before they flower. One weed you let go to seed will turn into thousands of more weeds next season. Pull it before it blooms.

Hoe. The work of hand-weeding is much easier with the right tools. A hoe has a long handle and a sharp edge designed to sever weeds stems from the roots just below the soil surface. You'll find lots of hoe designs to choose from. Forget about the square-headed traditional garden hoe for this job. Get yourself an oscillating or a swan neck hoe instead. To hoe your garden without cultivating a backache, hold the hoe like you are sweeping with a broom—that is, with the thumbs on both of your hands pointing up not down the handle. Skim the sharp sides of the hoe blade through the top inch of the soil and slice off the weeds. Do this several times to a weed and you can keep it from regrowing.

Weed-killing sprays. While you want to avoid chemical herbicides, you can find less toxic, more natural options for eliminating weeds with a spray. These formulas rely on vinegar, soap, clove, or citrus oil, or a combination of those ingredients to kill individual weeds. They work best when applied on a sunny day and often take multiple dousings before the weed is completely dead. These organic weed killers are not harmful to people, pets, or wildlife, but they do kill any plant they come in contact with, so don't let any get on the plants you are trying to grow. When spraying organic herbicides, create a spray shield from a soda bottle to spare surrounding plants and groundcovers. To do this cut off the bottom one-third of a two-liter soda bottle, place the top part of the bottle over the weed, and spray the herbicide into the bottle top. Lift the bottle and move on to the next plant when the herbicide drips down onto the weed.

Corn solution. In the 1980s, a scientist at Iowa State University made a discovery about corn gluten meal, a by-product of corn processing that is often used as food for livestock. He found that corn gluten meal inhibits seeds from germinating. Now you can buy corn gluten meal in bags (or in bulk at rural feed stores) and spread it on the soil to suppress weed seeds from sprouting. This works best early in the season because once the weeds have gone beyond the sprout stage, corn gluten does not affect them. Also, corn gluten doesn't discriminate between seeds you want to sprout and those you don't want, so if you are growing your crop by sowing seeds directly in the soil, corn gluten is not a smart choice for you.

Corn gluten does come with a bonus: a substantial supply of nitrogen, so it acts as a true "weed-and-feed" product, like the chemicals but not toxic. Again, spread it on your plot early in the season to give the soil microbes time to digest and release the nitrogen to your plants' roots.

Sun-baked. When you're just starting out or if your ideal plot is thick with weeds, you can enlist the sun's help to clean up the soil. The process, known as "solarization," aims to cook the weeds to death under plastic. It is easy, but requires you to leave the plot unplanted for several months during the growing season, which makes this technique useful only for the most unconquerable weed problems. The hotter and more humid the climate, the better this technique works.

To solarize your soil, start in late spring or early summer, and pull, hoe, or rake out as many weeds as you can from the bed. Then, moisten the soil and cover it with clear plastic, weighting or burying the edges. Leave the plastic in place for 6 weeks. Dampen the soil whenever it gets dry (you should see condensation on the plastic—if you don't, it's time to water the ground again). When you remove the plastic, all the weeds and weed seeds will be dead and you can plant.

QUICK HITS

- Pass on herbicides.
- Mulch early and often to block weeds.
- Pull small weeds frequently. Never let one go to seed.
- Organic sprays work on targeted plants.

Not Ready For Round-Up

The chemical herbicide most widely used by homeowners, gardeners, and farmers is sold under the brand-name Roundup, but scientifically speaking is called "glyphosate." By all accounts, it is less toxic and persistent in the environment than many other herbicides. It is also less toxic to people than earlier weed-killers were.

However, multiple studies have found that glysophate does reduce the populations of beneficial microbes in the soil and leaves the remaining ones less active. Applying Roundup to your organic cannabis plot negates all the smart, hard work you put in to building up the soil food chain and all the good it does for your plants. In Dr. Kindbud's estimation, that isn't worth the risk when you have other options for controlling weeds.

Remember Paraquat?

If you were a weed smoker in the 1970s, you probably remember paraquat. At that time, the U.S. government sponsored a program to spray the herbicide on marijuana fields in Mexico to kill the crop. It did not eliminate all the weed growing in Mexico and coming into the U.S., but the government encouraged the belief that smoking pot treated with paraquat would be dangerous to people and urged everyone to stay away from the crop.

Subsequent research has not found any link between smoking paraquat-treated pot and ill health effects in people. The residue appears to be converted to harmless compounds when burned on leaves. No injury or illness has been linked to smoking pot contaminated by paraquat.

Of course, ingesting pure paraquat is highly toxic to people and other mammals and there are no specific antidotes. In some parts of the developing world, the availability of paraquat has made it an all-too-common choice for desperate people who wish to commit suicide. Paraquat is still available in the United States, but only to licensed applicators. The U.S. government no longer sponsors the spraying of marijuana fields with the herbicide.

CHAPTER TEN

Bud Time

Now comes the moment you've been waiting for—harvesting bagfuls of your homegrown, pure and natural, organic, and very kind buds. While there's no reason not to sample a little of your harvest whenever you and it are ready, you also want to be patient to ensure that you get the majority of your buds at their peak and prepare them to be stored until you are ready to enjoy them.

When to Harvest

There is no exact date you can know on which your buds will be ready for picking. Not even in the same place, with the same variety planted at the same time and cared for in exactly the same way from one season to the next. Rather, you want to rely on a series of cues from the plant and the weather forecast that you observe and react to.

As the amount of daylight diminishes and the nights grow cooler, your plants' growth slows and then stops completely. Only focused attention and experience will tell you when this moment comes.

Take your time and be sure about this. The buds can add up to 25 percent of weight in the last two weeks of their growth. When they stop, the pistils, or "hairs" in the buds, become darker in color. Under ideal conditions—warm and dry for weeks on end--this is the moment to harvest your crop. In most parts of North America, the ideal conditions don't often occur at the end of the growing season. Falling temperatures and rain can push you to harvest sooner.

Flaky Frosts

When you started your crop, you needed to know the average last frost date in spring for your area. As I explained in Chapter 5, you can find that information online or by phone from your county extension office. At the other end of the season, harvest time, you need to know your area's average first frost date in fall.

A mild frost does not kill cannabis plants, but most of the time it shuts them down for the season, ending their further growth and development. If a warm, sunny spell is forecast after the light frost, you can leave the plants in the ground and they may continue to grow. But if the weather doesn't warm up after a light frost, pull the plants because they are finished growing.

A hard frost, when everything freezes, almost always kills the plants and can damage the buds. You want to be sure to harvest before a hard frost strikes.

Frost does not occur only when temperatures drop below freezing. Humidity and temperature in relation to each other create a dewpoint—the conditions at which the moisture will condense out of the air and become liquid on plants and car windows. Frost forms when the surface temperature (on leaves, glass, etc.) is near or below freezing and the air temperature falls to within a few degrees of the dewpoint. A mild frost can develop when the air temperature is 35 to 37 degrees, and under the right conditions even warmer.

Clear nights with a light wind are the most common conditions for frost formation. When frosts are likely, radio and TV weather forecasts report on it. But keep in mind that weather can be very, very local. Rural areas generally are cooler than cities, where asphalt and buildings radiate heat at night. Also, if your crop is growing on top of a slope (cold air flows downhill) or is protected from the wind by a hedgerow, it may be spared a few early frosts. If, on the other hand, your plot is at the bottom of a slope or especially exposed to the wind, then frost may hit your plants sooner. As your growing season winds down, be alert to the weather forecast and aware of your own unique conditions so you don't lose your crop.

You can sometimes get a few extra nights or even a week or two for your buds to mature by protecting them from frost by covering the plants through the first few mild frosts. Simply drape them with old sheets or blankets, or, if you got row cover in spring to protect your plants from pollination or pests, you can use that. Cover the plants about an hour before sunset. Watering the plants also helps reduce the risk of frost by increasing the humidity in the immediate area.

Rain Wreck

Fungus can spoil your harvest, turning fragrant, tasty buds into musty, hard-to-burn, funky schwag. Mold, mildew, and other fungi grow on plant surfaces that are constantly moist. You'll remember (or you should go back and check in Chapter 7) that I advised you to water your plants by directing the flow right onto the soil rather than on the plants. The reason is that it both uses water most efficiently and it protects the plants from fungal diseases.

If you've been following that advice, you've made sure that your soil drains well, and your summer weather has not been too rainy, your plants should be mostly fungus free. But late summer and early fall are often rainy in many parts of North America. A few rainy days can give fungi a toehold on your crop. So you need to watch the weather forecast and if your buds are close to being ready before a rainy spell is predicted, harvest them before they get soggy. The drier the plants are when you harvest them, the better your buds will taste and the longer they will keep in storage.

Autumn Awareness

Two other common fall occurrences can influence when you harvest your crop. First, as most other plants start to die down, your still-green, tall cannabis plants become much more visible. If you need to keep your crop discreet, you may have to harvest sooner rather than later.

Likewise, autumn is the season for hunting for deer, turkey, and other wildlife in many states. Hunters walking through fields may damage or plunder your crop. Check with your local game commission on when the hunting seasons begin and consider harvesting your crop before then.

Curing Cannabis

You can sample a few of your buds right after you harvest them. But to be sure the majority keep well until you are ready to enjoy them, take the time to cure them properly.

Green Weed

The Organic Guide To Growing High-Quality Cannabis

Start by pulling the whole plant out of the ground—roots and all. Hang the plants upside down for 48 hours in a cool, dry spot away from direct sunlight. Leave space between each plant and as much as possible ensure that air can flow around them on all sides.

After a couple of days, clip off the roots and stems up to the lowest set of leaves on each plant. (Toss the trimmings into your compost pile.) Put each top into its own paper grocery bag. Leave the bags wide open and store them in a cool, dry place away from direct sunlight. I hope you're getting the message that throughout the process of curing and storing your cannabis, the best location is cool (60 to 65 degrees Fahrenheit is ideal), low in humidity and protected from direct sunlight. Attics and garages are commonly used. Basements tend to be too damp.

When the plants have been in the bags for four to five days, clip the buds from the stems and trim off large "fan" leaves that may have formed around the buds. You could store the buds away at this stage. But if you are able to, spread them out on a screen (an old window screen works great for this) and leave them in your cool, dry location so that air can circulate around them on all sides. Leave them there for a couple of days and you can be sure they will be mold free.

Bud Storage

If you grew more than a couple plants and followed the guidance in this book, you probably have harvested more buds than you can use in a few weeks. After you have cured them thoroughly as described in the previous section, put them in glass jars—old-school Mason canning jars work great for this. If you don't have access to glass jars, you can also use plastic containers (like Tupperware) or even plastic bags. Whichever you use, seal them tightly and keep them in—you guessed it—a cool, dry place away from direct sunlight. Check on them periodically, especially in the first few weeks, to be sure there's no condensation on the container

(which can encourage mold to form) or worse, a musty smell that indicates mildew has already formed. If you do find condensation or mildew forming, remove the buds from the jar or bag and set them on a screen for two to three days to finish drying them out.

Smoke Right

How you enjoy your harvest is, of course, a matter of personal preference. Since you took the trouble to grow an organic crop, you probably want to enjoy it as naturally as possible. I have just a few thoughts about that.

For rolling joints, you can't beat sheer, glueless papers like the Club brand. They have no burning adhesive or dense fibers that can overpower the taste of your great buds.

Glass lets the pure and complex flavors of your organic buds come through untainted. Wooden and even metal pipes have their own taste, particularly after they've been used for a long time. Same goes for screens. A glass bowl or bong (water pipe) needs no screen, is easy to keep clean and never tastes like anything but weed.

I don't know how much butane you inhale over years of lighting up with disposable cigarette lighters, but even a little is not as good as none. Instead, use matches, especially wooden matches, whenever you can.

You already know you should not drive a car or operate heavy machinery after smoking pot, right? But what should you do?

Watch a movie. I'm not into horror movies, but the freakier the film the better it is when you're high.

Take a hike. The rhythm of walking can give your mind the release to wander and ponder, the gift that smoking weed gives you. Also, observing nature and how it functions in every season helps you to become a better grower.

Listen To Music

Listen to music. All by itself, music can alter your mood and your consciousness. Teamed with a good buzz—from weed you grew yourself—music can carry you outside your body or into the depths of your mind. Five favorites of mine for stoned listening:

Grateful Dead • Wilco • Miles Davis • Sonny Rollins • Phllip Glass

MELODY MAKERS
The Trip
STEEL PULSE
1 STUD
CD-1036A
One Love
(Bob Marley)
Bob Marley
RECORDED BY JAMAICA RECORDING STUDIO 13 BRENTFO

The Organic Guide To Growing High-Quality Cannabis

Lie in a hammock or sit under a tree. Now tune into nature, smell the fresh air, feel the warm sensation of sunshine on your face, hear the buzz of every living thing going about its business. Cool.

QUICK HITS

- Let the plants grow as long as possible. They add a lot of weight in the final weeks.
- Protect your plants from a mild frost, harvest before a hard frost.
- Pick before a heavy rainstorm.
- Cure and store your buds in a cool, dry place.

A tip from Dr. Kindbud: Wear gloves when handling the stalks and buds to minimize the amount of THC-loaded resin that ends up on your hands.

CHAPTER ELEVEN

Farming Indoors

Do you live in the **Far North**, where the growing season is too short for a cannabis crop to fully mature outside? Want to grow year-round? Are you in a city or other place where there is no available land? Do you need to keep your crop secure from unwanted attention?

A truly organic crop needs sunshine, rain, fresh air, and real living soil. Still, you can grow a healthy crop of cannabis indoors without using toxic chemicals. Much of the information in this book still applies to growing inside, but you do need to pay special attention to lighting, ventilation and humidity, soil and containers, watering and fertilizing.

Right Lighting

Sunshine provides your plants with the full-spectrum of light, from the ultraviolet to the infrared and all the frequencies in between. This is the type of light they've evolved with, that they rely on for photosynthesis and flowering. A greenhouse is an ideal indoor growing environment because it exposes your plants

to the maximum available sunlight while protecting them from other outdoor elements. Ventilation is the most critical concern for greenhouse growers—on sunny days when the outdoor temperature is warmer than about 75 degrees Fahrenheit, the temperature inside a greenhouse can soar past 100 degrees Fahrenheit, hot enough to wilt your plants and perhaps even permanently damage them. Be sure to open windows or run fans in your greenhouse on warm, sunny days. Even in a greenhouse, you'll have to supply supplemental light to grow during the winter months.

You don't need a greenhouse, though, to grow indoors. But the amount of sunlight your plants get—even in a bright, sunny room that faces south or west—is not sufficient for them to grow up healthy and mature. You must provide supplemental lighting and manage it carefully to get your plants to complete their life cycle and produce buds for you to enjoy.

For starting seeds, ordinary fluorescent fixtures and light bulbs work well, but they're not powerful enough for growing mature plants. Incandescent lights (like your standard household light bulbs) are stronger, but they tend to get hot and, because you can't put the plants close without burning them, you get long stems that are spindly, weak, and prone to toppling over. For raising full-grown plants with lush foliage that eventually flower, you need to invest in lights designed specifically for raising plants inside.

You can get fluorescent bulbs for growing plants, which are strong in the red and blue ends of the light spectrum. Many growers find that they work fine. But for maximum productivity, you want to use either metal halide or high-pressure sodium lamps. Metal halide lamps are strong on the blue side of the spectrum. If your growing room gets little or no natural light, metal halide is almost essential. The sodium lights work great as a supplement to natural light. Their strength in the red-orange end of the spectrum helps promote flowering and budding. If at all possible, get both types of lights—the extra cost will be paid back in a bigger, better harvest.

On the Screen:

Movies featuring cannabis
Dazed and Confused
Fast Times at Ridgmont High
Harold and Kumar Go to White Castle
Humboldt
Knocked Up
Pieces of April
Reefer Madness
Saving Grace
Up In Smoke
The Wackness
Where the Buffalo Roam

Artificial lights work best when they are as close to the plants as can be. As your plants grow, keep the top leaves two to three inches from the lights. Experienced indoor growers often hang the lights from adjustable chains, but you can also set up your pots on shelves or platforms that can be raised or lowered to keep the plants close to the light. This is crucial because when the lights are too far from the plants, they put all of their energy into growing longer stems to get closer. You want shorter plants that focus their energy on growing leaves and then flowering, not on lengthening their stems.

Controlling how much light your plants get is vitally important indoors because there is no natural cycle for the plants to follow. If you want to harvest buds, you must pay strict attention to the light and dark periods. As the plants are building their stems, branches, and leaves, you want to give them as much light as you can—up to 24 hours a day, if possible. If you need to shut off the lights each day to save money or for any other reason, be sure they get at least 14 hours of light daily. Give them the maximum amount of light for at least three months so the plant can make a dense canopy of branches and leaves. The older and bigger the plant is when it starts to flower, the more buds it will produce and they will be more potent. When you're ready for budding to begin, increase the dark period to more than 10 hours daily. As I explained in Chapter 6, the change in the light-dark cycle triggers flowering.

Attaching a timer to the lights is almost essential for managing this properly. If you are inconsistent with the amount of light, some of the plants may flower, others may not. This could interfere with your chances of separating the males from the females, and can even cause all of them to become hermaphrodites, leaving you with few buds and lots of seeds. Also, don't let light of any kind break up the dark period—streetlights outside a window or even a flashlight can be enough to disrupt the process. Make sure the room is sealed off from any ambient light and take care not to open the door when the room is dark.

Air and Heat

Your grow room needs to be closed to light, but it cannot be shut off from air. Plants take in air, use the carbon dioxide, and emit oxygen. (People, you may recall, do the opposite.) A steady supply of fresh carbon dioxide is essential for healthy plant growth. In a closet or small room, a table-size fan and your respiration can be enough to meet your plants' needs. In a large room or greenhouse, a ventilation fan that draws in fresh air and pushes out the stale air makes a big difference. Plants that are not getting enough fresh air turn yellow and droop.

The ideal temperature for your indoor plants is between 68 and 78 degrees Fahrenheit, with a 10 to 15 degree drop during the dark hours. This is close to normal for most homes. Getting the humidity level right can be trickier. Dry conditions cause the plants to produce THC-rich resin on the leaves to conserve moisture. In a humid environment, cannabis leaves grow wide and don't produce much resin. When you water your plants, the humidity level in the room naturally increases. The light breeze from a fan can help dry out plants in a small room. Set up a dehumidifier in a large room.

A tip from Dr. Kindbud: Before you buy nursery pots, ask professional landscapers and home gardeners for any used ones they are planning to discard.

The Organic Guide To Growing High-Quality Cannabis

Soil and Containers

Plants growing in the ground outside enjoy the benefits of a healthy, self-sustaining soil microbe population to nurture and nourish them. Indoors, you want to do all you can to mimic those conditions.

That does not mean, however, that you should use soil from outside to grow plants in containers, indoors or out. It is too heavy, holding so much moisture that the plants may drown. Instead, mix equal parts of peat moss or coir (the fibers left behind from the processing of coconuts) and fully decomposed compost. The peat or coir ensures that the mix is light enough to drain well, the compost provides nutrients and holds moisture just long enough to disperse it evenly to the roots.

Start your plants in small containers, like the seedling containers I described in Chapter 5, or even used yogurt cups. Be sure there are drainage holes in the bottom of any container you choose. As the plants grow, move them up to larger pots, eventually to 10-gallon plastic nursery containers. Put only the soil mix in the pots. No pebbles, packing peanuts, broken pottery, or anything else that takes up root space. Some growers claim that this helps the soil drain better, but it has been proven that holes are sufficient, and the plants need all the room to grow roots you can give them. Stay away from "watering crystals," too. Not only are they not natural, they give a false sense of security. Compost can manage the moisture if you provide it regularly.

Watering and Feeding

One advantage indoor growers have over most outdoor crops is in providing a constant water supply. Just be careful not to overwater, which can drown the plant or set up conditions for fungus to take hold. Push your finger into the soil down to your second knuckle. If you feel the soil is damp at that level, hold off on watering.

When you do need to water, the best place to deliver it is from below. Sit your pots in a dish of water and then let the water wick up to the roots. If you can't do that, at the least be sure to pour the water directly on the soil and not on the leaves. Just like outside, it is better to give the plants a good dousing once or twice a week than a little sprinkle each day. When the soil at the bottom of the pot is damp, roots grow down to extract the water. If the water is only in the top couple inches, the roots stay shallow. The bigger the root system, the bigger the plant. The bigger the plant, the more buds you will harvest.

You can buy drip irrigation systems specifically for growing in containers. Add a timer and you have an almost attention-free system that gives your plants a steady supply of moisture.

The compost in your soil mix provides a healthy dose of nutrients. But as your plant grows, it needs more. Get liquid fish and seaweed fertilizer (sold under brand names such as Neptune's Harvest and Alaska), which you mix with water. Start with a dilute solution, as little as just a teaspoon in a quart of water, and gradually increase it to the proportions recommended on the package. Feed your plants with this just once a week—excess fertilizer disrupts the plants' natural growth pattern. When flowering begins, switch to a fertilizer that is higher in phosphorus—BioBloom is a widely available brand.

QUICK HITS

- Use lights made for indoor plant growing
- Manage the light and dark cycle carefully
- Keep the room dry and well-ventilated
- Use a soil mix for containers, not soil dug up outside
- Keep moisture constant but beware of overwatering

Hydroponic Organic - Not

Hydroponics is the cultivation of plants in nutrient-rich water rather than in soil. I've heard growers—of vegetables as well as cannabis—say they are growing a hydroponic crop organically. You can certainly use organically-based liquid fertilizers rather than synthetic ones in a hydroponic system, and that would be better than pumping the plants full of manufactured nitrates.

A truly organic crop, however, can only be grown in soil. A hydroponic system is unnatural—the plants did not evolve to grow in water—and it does not include the beneficial microbes in the soil that have a symbiotic relationship with the plants. The hydroponic grower takes nutrients but does not replenish them. An organic grower nurtures an ecosystem that encompasses the plants' whole life cycle, from germination to growth to maturation to decay to regeneration, and supports all of the organisms that interact with the plant.

If you need to grow indoors, at least get your plants in soil. And the next time someone tells you they are doing "organic hydroponic" remember there really is no such thing.

CHAPTER TWELVE

Trouble-Shooting Guide

You chose to grow organic because you know that's best for your plants, yourself, your family and pets, and every other living thing on Earth. If you've followed the advice in this book, you have created the conditions in which your plants naturally grow healthy and strong enough to overcome most any threat to their well-being. Yes, there can at times be problems that require your intervention, but go for the least-invasive, nontoxic solutions to protect your crop and the planet.

Bugs and Other Creepy Crawlies

The first reaction many gardeners and cannabis cultivators have when they see insects around their plants is to do everything possible to get rid of the bugs. But did you know that 80 percent or more of all insects are actually beneficial to plants? Many are essential for pollinating—not only bees, but moths, beetles, and others play a critical role in producing the fruits and vegetables we all love to munch on. Insects such as the ladybug and praying mantis prey on other insects, eating up thousands of pests each

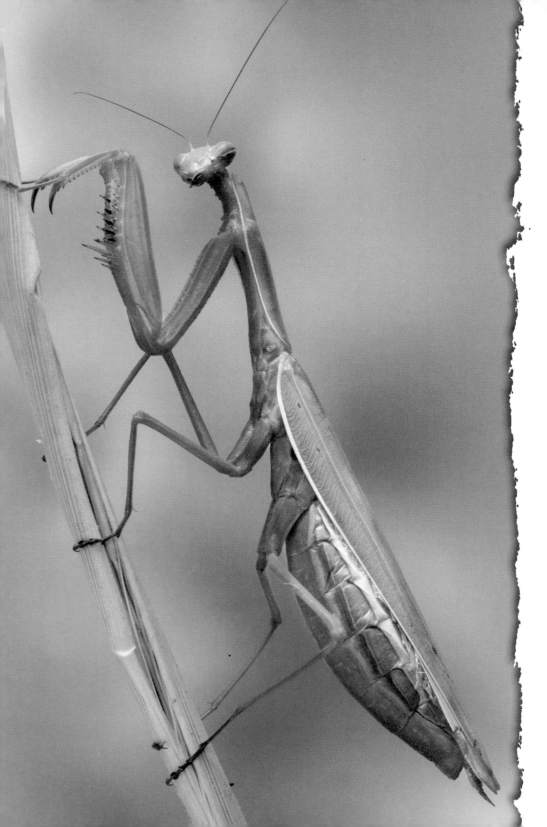

day. Quite a few other insects may live and feed around plants, but never damage them. One more good reason not to use chemical pesticides: they kill good bugs and bad ones alike, and in that way can knock them out of balance, which can lead to more pests and the need for more drastic measures.

Before you react, then, take the time to observe the insects around your plants. Are they damaging the plants or just hanging around them? If there is damage, is it extensive or just a few holes in the leaves, which your healthy, well-fed plants can outgrow?

Even if the plants are being chewed, wait before you react. In a balanced ecosystem—like your organic cannabis plot—the predatory insects tend to be in the area or are attracted to it by the presence of their food supply. By the way, many of the most voracious consumers of pests are tiny wasps and flies, which you might think are just more pests.

Attracting and keeping predatory insects near your plot is as easy as planting flowers, such as low-growing sweet alyssum, and herbs like dill around it. The insects need the nectar from flowers to supplement their diet of bugs. Put a small dish of water in the area, too, because the predators need water. While you're at it, add a birdbath, if you can, because birds eat bugs and feed them to their young as well. They come to drink and wash in the birdbath, they stay to chow down on pest insects in your plot. Lizards and toads are helpful consumers of pests, too, so count yourself lucky if a few are hanging around your pot patch.

Nine times out of ten, the predators and pests get into balance with each other and your plants will be problem free. But what if your plot is infested with pests that are damaging your plants? Must organic growers simply watch as all of their time and effort are destroyed by pests? No, you just have to choose a remedy that is targeted at the specific pests and harms nothing but the pests.

The Organic Guide To Growing High-Quality Cannabis

Start by making sure you have a positive identification of the pest, so that you can select the right treatment. You can find many good books to help with this or visit one of the Websites listed in this book's Resources section. Once you know what pest you are dealing with, you can choose one of the following solutions to apply:

Water. Yes, plain old H_20, applied with a forceful stream, can knock pests like aphids off plants. They can't climb back on in their flightless, plant-eating nymph stage (they're on your plants because they hatched from eggs laid on the plants), so they're done sucking the sap from leaves and stems.

Spider mites are tiny pests that hide on the underside of leaves and chew on them. The mites favor very dry conditions, so give your plants a thorough rinse if they become infested with the little buggers.

Barriers. Blocking pests' access to your plants is a simple and otherwise harmless approach. Row covers, which I recommended for protecting your plants from cold and unwanted pollination, also can defend your full-grown plants from flying insects.

Crawling cutworms feed on seedlings, especially at the just-sprouted-from-seed stage. You can form little "collars" for seedlings out of scrap cardboard or stiff paper. Wrap the collars around the base of your plants, bury the bottom of the collars a half-inch or so deep in the soil, and they will thwart cutworms.

When and where the conditions are consistently damp, slugs and snails can be troublesome. You can find in garden centers and online many products targeted at those slimy pests. Diatomaceous Earth, made from sharp-edged fossils, slices open the slugs' soft bodies when they crawl through it. Spread it around your plants to stop the slugs before they get to them. Be sure to get DE produced

for this purpose and not the kind made for use in swimming pool filters. And remember to reapply it after every rainstorm, when the slugs are at their most active. Beer traps are a less expensive approach to dealing with slugs. Bury small plastic tubs (like margarine comes in) so that the rim is even with the soil. Then just dump the dregs from your bottle, can, glass, or keg into the tub each night and collect the besotted slimers in it each morning (they are attracted to the yeast).

Traps. You can capture and dispose of flying pests using sticky traps. You might be familiar with the "bag-a-bug" beetle traps that many homeowners use. Those traps have a pheromone lure to attract the beetles, which fall into the bag and can't get out. Sticky traps are typically small squares of plastic or cardboard with an adhesive applied. When the bugs hit the glue, they're stuck. These are particularly effective against whiteflies, which are a common problem when you're growing inside.

Soap. The long chain fatty acids in soap wash away insects' protective outer coating and disrupt their normal functions. Insecticidal soap is effective against soft-bodied insects such as aphids and thrips, as well as spider mites and immature leafhoppers. The soap has to come in direct contact with the pests to work; that is, you can't just spray it on the leaves, you have to hit the pests with it. You can buy specially formulated insecticidal soap products in garden centers or online. Many growers find that a tablespoon of ordinary liquid dish soap (like Dawn) mixed into a quart of water, with a teaspoon of cooking oil added to help it stick, works as well as the special soap.

Oil. Scale are almost invisible on your plants and if you do see them you might mistake them for a disease. These nearly immobile insects attach themselves to plant stems, adopt the color, and then start to swell and consume the plants. If you find what look like nubby, swollen growths and identify them as scale, the surest treatment is spraying them with horticultural oil. Be sure to get

The Organic Guide To Growing High-Quality Cannabis

a "light" or "summer" oil (rather than dormant oil) to avoid damaging your plants as you eliminate the scale.

Bacteria. Caterpillars are not known to plague pot plants, but if they do show up on yours, you can use a naturally occurring bacteria, known as *Bacillus thuringiensis* or Bt, to control them. It comes in a liquid or powder you mix with water and then spray on your plants. It is harmless to people, songbirds, and everything but caterpillars. When it chews leaves treated with Bt, the caterpillar digestive tract is damaged and it is soon dead.

Four-legged Fiends

The most troublesome pests for many growers are not the kind with six or eight legs or even wings. Wildlife including deer, woodchucks (a.k.a. groundhogs), and rabbits, do, in some places, munch on cannabis plants, especially in early spring when the plants are tender and other food is scarce. Protecting your crop from these critters does not, however, require a shotgun or poisonous chemicals.

A fence is the most reliable way to keep wildlife away from your crop. An electric fence works best of all—it will also impede any two-legged varmints with a mind to get at your crop. A fence needs to be at least eight feet high to be tall enough so that deer won't try to jump it. Even better if it's angled inward, because deer won't jump where they're not sure of the landing. For woodchucks and

rabbits, bury the fence a foot or two underground—otherwise, they'll tunnel under it.

If you're growing where a fence isn't feasible, you can try to scare wildlife away with whirligigs (which spin when blown by the wind), reflector tape, motion-detector lights or sprinklers, or just about anything else that moves or glitters enough to unnerve the animals. The more of these you use, the more effective they'll be, because over time the animals grow accustomed to them and are no longer spooked by them. At least, mix them up so that the change gives the marauders pause before they decide to eat your crop.

Certain aromas can also deter wildlife from your patch. Many gardeners find that hanging bars of strong-smelling soap, like Irish Spring, by string tied to low branches of trees and other plants discourages deer from walking through the area. Homemade sprays produced by blending hot peppers, garlic, and even rotten eggs and then appling them to leaves can stop critters from chewing on a plant. You can buy specially formulated deer repellents that have the same effect.

Another product you can buy is fox urine (in liquid concentrate or powder)—no, I am not making this up—that you sprinkle around the perimeter of your plot to scare off critters with the scent of a

The Organic Guide To Growing High-Quality Cannabis

predator. If you have a dog, it might serve the same purpose. In fact, distribute a bit of your own "scent" around the area and it's likely to work, too.

I hate to be discouraging, but you sometimes have to accept what nature wants. If you're growing where the critter population is high and your plants are the best available food source, they will eat your plants no matter what you do. You need to find a new location for your plot if your plants have been munched to the ground more than once.

Damaging Diseases

Unless you're growing acres and acres of cannabis, you're not likely to have to deal with serious plant diseases often. If all of a sudden most of your plants wither, wilt, or turn brown, they may have been stricken by blight or another fast-spreading virus. There are no treatments—organic or otherwise—for plants struck by viruses like those. Pull out every afflicted plant and dispose of it far away from any that are still growing.

Plant diseases are mostly soilborne—that is, the organisms that cause diseases (called pathogens) live and reproduce in the soil. The key to preventing them from infecting your plants is to nurture the beneficial soil microbes with a steady supply of organic matter to digest. A robust population of good microbes monopolizes the available nutrients and neutralizes the pathogens. In some situations even the beneficial microbes can't ward off an especially strong or resilient pathogen invasion. If you have the same problems from year to year, the soil has become infected and you need to look for a new location.

Seedlings started indoors may be afflicted by a quick-moving fungal disease called "damping off." It can show up literally overnight and wilt seedlings that looked healthy just hours before. Damping off is particularly common in humid environments. If a few of your seedlings have been hit by it, sprinkle dry peat moss or

cornmeal on top of the soil, where the fungus forms.

Where humidity is constantly high—in coastal climates, for instance—fungus tends to grow and spread on cannabis plants. At around the midpoint of the buds' development, they become susceptible to "bud rot," turning them dark brown and mushy to the touch. It is very destructive and highly contagious (to plants, not to people). Protect your other buds by removing the whole branch on which an infected bud grows, not just the affected piece of the bud. Handle the rotting bud carefully—you don't want to do anything that will cause more fungal spores to be released into the air and onto healthy plants. Wash your hands after handling affected plants so you don't risk infecting others when you touch them.

Malnutrition

Plants growing in rich organic soil and fed with natural, slow-release fertilizers are healthy and strong enough to fend off most pests and diseases. When plants don't have all the nutrients they need available to them, they are not only more vulnerable to other problems, they may develop symptoms that can appear to be caused by a disease or pest.

As you can't help but have noticed, soil chemistry is complex. Nutrients must be both present in the soil and available to the plants. When the pH is too high or too low, or when each element is not in balance with the others—for instance, too much calcium vs. magnesium—the plant can't take up and use all the nutrients it needs.

Here is a list of some of the common signs of malnutrition:
• Yellow leaves, especially lower on the plant, red stems and stunted growth are caused by a nitrogen and/or phosphorus deficiency.

• When the plants fail to form flowers, they are most likely short on phosphorus.

• Calcium deficient plants are very slow-growing and stunted.
• Insufficient sulfur shows when new growth is yellow rather than green
• Without enough magnesium, leaves curl up.

Leaves lacking iron are pale, but the veins are still dark.

You might hear about quick fixes for these deficiencies, even organic ones like the soil amendments I recommended in Chapter 3, but they're not your real answer. Plants grow best feeding on nutrients delivered in the way they've evolved to use them. You need to feed the soil microbes a steady diet of organic matter, which they digest into all the nutrients needed in exactly the right balance. It's simple, and it's guaranteed to work. I realize the quick fixes are tempting—it's easier, though, to create more imbalance than to remedy it. Instead, build your soil season after season and your plants will grow with few, if any, problems every year.

A tip from Dr. Kindbud: Where critters like deer and groundhogs are a pest, try planting a trap crop like big leafy heads of kale and cabbage, which they will prefer to eat instead of your cannabis plants.

QUICK HITS

• Observe pests before you react.
• Scare off varmints with motion.
• Rip out diseased plants fast.
• Undernourished plants may look diseased.
• Resist the quick fix.

CHAPTER THIRTEEN

Graduate Level

Once you've mastered the basics of cannabis growing, you are ready to try a few advanced strategies and techniques that may help you get more out of the experience.

Cover Your Assets

Soil amendments, fertilizers, and even compost are relatively quick fixes for soil that is less than perfect. To build the ideal medium that will yield the healthiest and most productive plants for years to come, use the method that farmers and other expert organic growers rely on: cover cropping. During the off-season, you grow plants in your plot that improve the soil's fertility, texture, and beneficial microbe population, and prevent weeds from taking over. When you are ready to plant in the spring, you cut or knock down the cover crop, which adds even more valuable organic matter to the soil.

Cover crops plants tend to be one of two types. Legumes (beans are familiar members of this family) have the unique property of drawing nitrogen out of the air and "fixing" it in the soil. To build fertile soil, plant legumes such as Austrian peas, hairy vetch, and

crimson clover. Grasses, which include grain plants, produce deep roots that loosen soil, dredge up minerals from deep in the soil, and produce loads of organic matter. Cereal rye and oats are popular choices for small garden plots. Buckwheat is the fastest growing cover crop, and its white flowers look nice and attract pollinating bees. When growing any kind of grass or grain, be sure to cut them down (use a weed wacker, hedge shears, or a classic scythe) before they produce seeds, which generally happens shortly after they flower, or they are likely to replant themselves and become a weed problem for you to deal with.

Seeds for these "green manures" are available at farm-supply stores and online. They are often sold in bulk quantities better suited to farms than garden-size plots, in which case you may want to find another grower to share with you.

Cutting to Add

In ideal growing conditions, your cannabis plants could grow up to 20 feet tall during their four to six month growing season. Plants that tall may attract unwanted attention, but that's not the only reason for trimming them back. Pruning makes the stems stronger, and stimulates the plant to produce more of the sticky resin (where the THC resides) and more branches full of leaves that will yield more buds.

You may be reluctant at first to cut back plants you've worked hard to keep alive for weeks, but make yourself do it. You'll see they grow back fast—at the height of summer, they can grow 2.5 inches taller each day.

Start pruning them when the plants are about 18 inches tall. Get a pair of bypass pruners—if you're committed to growing a cannabis crop each year, the better-quality tools (such as Felco or Corona) are worth it. Sure, you could use a pair of paper scissors, a knife, or a razor blade, but a ragged cut can injure the plant or invite disease to infect it. Good tools produce better results.

Snip off the top leaf cluster or two on each of the plant's main limbs. Make your cut at a spot just above where two branches are on opposite sides of the stem. Slice as cleanly as possible. Repeat this twice more at two to three week intervals. If you don't see two or more new top branches forming after you cut, don't repeat because the plant isn't getting enough sunlight to sustain more leaf growth.

The compost pile isn't the only place to recycle your plant trimmings. You can turn them into clones, which is also an easy way to grow a back-up crop as a safeguard if the original doesn't survive.

Cloning

Planting your cannabis crop from seeds is smart when you're just starting out because seeds are accessible and unless you saved them all from one stash, they are likely to come from different strains and varieties. After you've grown them, you will discover which perform the best in your conditions. When you have identified a variety that really suits your needs, you can clone it.

Facts & Figures

80 million Americans admit having smoked marijuana.
20 million Americans smoked marijuana during the past year.
162 million people worldwide use cannabis in an average year.
Marijuana was first federally prohibited in 1937.
2.2 million pounds of marijuana were produced domestically in 1981.
22 million pounds of marijuana were produced domestically in 2006.
Cannabis is one of the top 3 cash crops in 30 states.

You don't need a lab or gene-splicing skills to do this. Simply snip off a limb from the top of the plant, just as I described in the preceding section on pruning. Then put the cut end of each cutting into a small pot filled with the seed-planting mix recommended in Chapter 5. Set the cuttings where they can get direct sunlight or put them under fluorescent lights about two to three inches away from the bulbs. Keep the soil mix consistently moist. Within a few days, the plant will start growing and within a week you'll notice it's taller and is beginning to add new leaves. The clones quickly catch up in size to the mother plants. In about three weeks, you can transplant them outside.

Extending the Season

A greenhouse is the most reliable way to extend your growing season. You can find moderately priced, easy-to-assemble kits made from aluminum and plastic sheeting that work almost as well as the very expensive (and very cool) wood and glass models. In a greenhouse with supplemental lighting, you can grow almost year-round.

A cold frame is a less costly approach that gives you an extra month or so of growing time at the beginning of the season. It is a box that rests on the ground and has a clear (usually glass) lid. The plants inside are protected from cold weather, especially at night, but get lots of sunlight during the day. You can buy a cold frame or make one from a discarded window and scrap wood. You can put your seedlings inside the cold frame a few weeks before the last frost date, giving them an invaluable head start on the season.

Whether you use a greenhouse or a cold frame, you want to orient it for the maximum light—that is, facing south or west. You also need to be very alert to ventilation. Both heat up in direct sun and your plants can cook inside them on a cool but sunny day. Open windows or the lid of your cold frame on any bright day.

Hemp vs. Marijuana

Hemp and marijuana both come from the Cannabis sativa plant. Hemp contains compounds that block the psychoactive effects of the plant. Instead, its value is as a source of food and fiber, for which it has been grown throughout the world for thousands of years.

At this time, more than 30 nations (including the United Kingdom and Canada) permit industrial hemp farming. In fact, the European Union subsidizes farmers who grow the crop. However, current law in the United States prohibits commercial hemp production without a federal license.

Still, you will find an increasing number of hemp products available even in the United States, from apparel and shoes to food products and even vitamins.

Plant A Garden

I understand that your primary interest may be in growing cannabis. But there are a number of benefits that will improve your cannabis crop if you plant vegetables, cooking herbs, and flowers, too:

• Nature does not monocrop, or grow just one type of plant in a particular space. A diverse planting is much less prone to problems with pests and diseases than a monocrop.
• Flowers and herbs attract a wide variety of beneficial insects (like those I described in Chapter 12), which help manage your pest problems.
• A garden full of many different plants is much less conspicuous than a stand of nothing but cannabis.
• The more you grow, the more you interact with and observe nature's processes, the better grower you will become. Gardening is an endless learning process and that's rewarding all on its own.
• There's a real thrill that comes from eating and sharing fresh and juicy organic food you've grown yourself. And when you reduce the distance your food travels to your plate, you lighten your impact on the environment and help make the world healthier and greener.

You already have most of the information you need to grow vegetables, herbs, and flowers, because the basics of soil and bed preparation, seed-starting and transplanting, watering and feeding, and weed and pest control that you've already read in this book apply whether you are growing tomatoes, lettuce, or cannabis. Some vegetables, herbs, and flowers grow best from seeds, others are more easily managed from transplants. Here's a rough breakdown:

Best grown from seeds: Beans, Beets, Carrots, Corn, Peas, Radishes, Spinach

Best grown from started plants: Basil, Broccoli, Cucumbers, Melons, Peppers, Squash, Tomatoes

Your choice: Lettuce and other salad greens

Resources

Seeds

I have never purchased seeds from any of these vendors nor do I have any relationship with them, so I am not recommending them. They are provided simply to give you a few leads if you are looking to buy.

Buy Dutch Seeds:
buydutchseeds.com

Ganja-seeds.com

Weed Seed Shop:
weedseedshop.com

Supplies for Organic Growers

Clean Air Gardening:
cleanairgardening.com
Compost bins, rain barrels, pest control

Composters.com
Compost bins, worm bins, rain barrels, season extenders

Dirtworks: dirtworks.net
Pest control, fertilizers, bagged compost

DripWorks:
dripworksusa.com
Drip irrigation systems and supplies

Extremely Green:
extremelygreen.com
Pest and weed control, fertilizers

Gardens Alive:
gardensalive.com
Pest control, fertilizers

Hydrofarm:
hydrofarm.com
Lights, greenhouses, nursery containers, and soil mixes

Morton's Horticultural Products: mortonproducts.com
Nursery containers, greenhouses, and accessories

Peaceful Valley Farm Supply:
groworganic.com
Soil amendments, cover crop seeds, pest and weed control, season extenders

Planet Natural:
planetnatural.com
Pest control, composters, fertilizers

Pest Identification
Bugguide.net

Insectidentification.org

Insect Identification Laboratory
at Virginia Tech:
idlab.ento.vt.edu

More Information on Growing Cannabis
Cannabis.com

Forum.grasscity.com
(community)

Growkind.com

High Times magazine:
hightimes.com

Medicalmarijuana.ca

Weedfarmer.com

Legal information on Growing Cannabis
Marijuana Policy Project:
mpp.org

National Organization for
Reform of Marijuana Laws
(NORML): norml.org

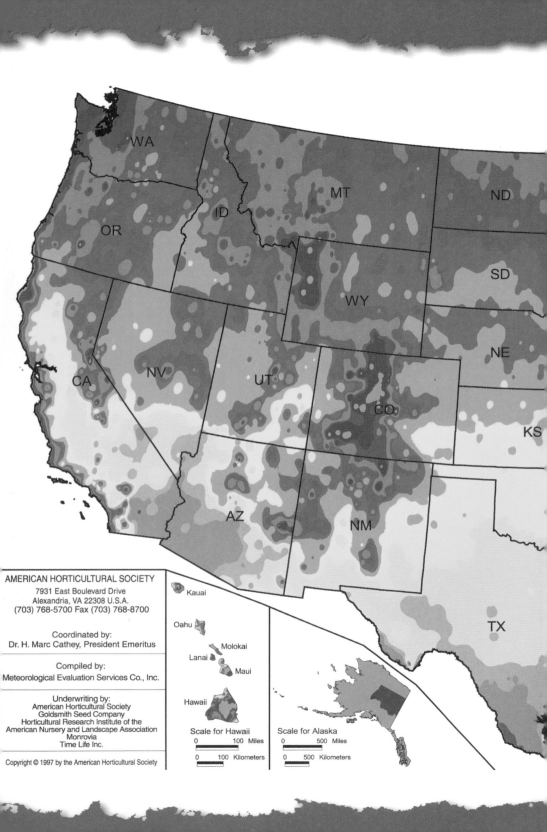

WA

OR

ID

MT

ND

SD

WY

NE

NV

UT

CO

KS

CA

AZ

NM

TX

AMERICAN HORTICULTURAL SOCIETY
7931 East Boulevard Drive
Alexandria, VA 22308 U.S.A.
(703) 768-5700 Fax (703) 768-8700

Coordinated by:
Dr. H. Marc Cathey, President Emeritus

Compiled by:
Meteorological Evaluation Services Co., Inc.

Underwriting by:
American Horticultural Society
Goldsmith Seed Company
Horticultural Research Institute of the
American Nursery and Landscape Association
Monrovia
Time Life Inc.

Copyright © 1997 by the American Horticultural Society

Kauai

Oahu

Molokai

Lanai

Maui

Hawaii

Scale for Hawaii

0   100 Miles

0   100 Kilometers

Scale for Alaska

0   500 Miles

0   500 Kilometers

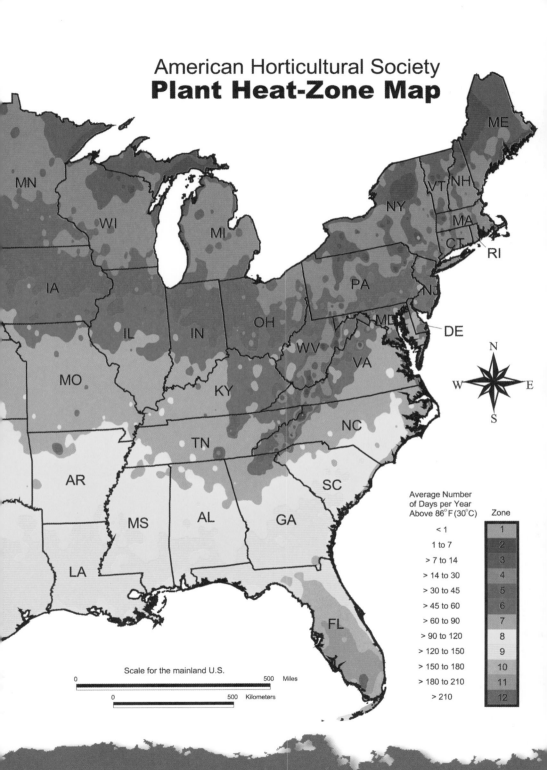

American Horticultural Society
Plant Heat-Zone Map

Average Number of Days per Year Above 86°F (30°C)	Zone
< 1	1
1 to 7	2
> 7 to 14	3
> 14 to 30	4
> 30 to 45	5
> 45 to 60	6
> 60 to 90	7
> 90 to 120	8
> 120 to 150	9
> 150 to 180	10
> 180 to 210	11
> 210	12

Scale for the mainland U.S.

0   500 Miles

0   500 Kilometers

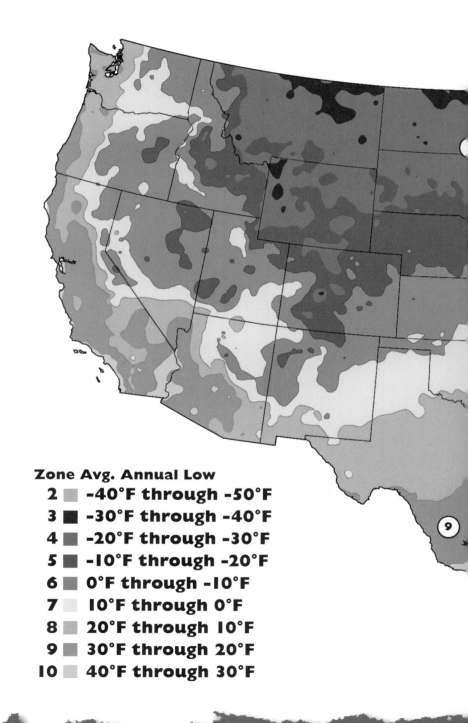

Zone Avg. Annual Low

2 ☐ -40°F through -50°F
3 ■ -30°F through -40°F
4 ■ -20°F through -30°F
5 ■ -10°F through -20°F
6 ■ 0°F through -10°F
7 ☐ 10°F through 0°F
8 ■ 20°F through 10°F
9 ■ 30°F through 20°F
10 ☐ 40°F through 30°F

Hardiness Zones Map

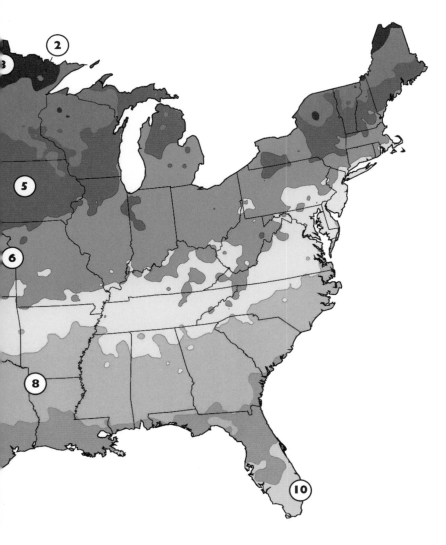

Go to arborday.org to find
the zone for your zip code.

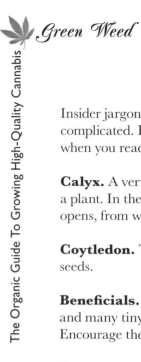
Glossary

Insider jargon can be baffling and makes even simple things sound complicated. But if you get to know these terms, you will be in the know when you read books and Websites, and talk to expert growers.

Calyx. A very thin membrane that surrounds the reproductive organs of a plant. In the case of cannabis, it is the visible outside of a flower before it opens, from which the pistils appear.

Coytledon. The tiny embryonic leaves that are the first to emerge from seeds.

Beneficials. Good bugs—not an oxymoron. Ladybugs, green lacewings, and many tiny wasps and flies prey on pests that damage your plants. Encourage these beneficials and avoid pesticides so you don't kill them.

Compost. A decomposed mix of yard waste, kitchen scraps, animal manure, and other ingredients. Known to organic gardeners as "black gold" because it nourishes plants, conditions soil, suppresses plant diseases, and manages moisture.

Dehiscence. Shedding of pollen by males.

Direct sowing. Planting seeds right in garden beds, rather than starting them indoors or in pots first.

Feminized seed. When a male plant is treated with an artificial hormone called gibberellic acid, it produces pollen with only "X" or female chromosomes. When a female plant is exposed to pollen with the X chromosome, it produces only female, or feminized, seed.

Humus. Partially decomposed organic matter. Humus is most often used to describe plant waste that naturally falls into place, such as tree leaves and pine needles, rather than that added by a grower.

Hybrid. A variety that results from cross-breeding two other varieties for particular characteristics, such as pest resistance or size. Seeds saved and replanted from a hybrid are not certain to have the same attributes as the parent plant.

N-P-K. The chemical symbols for nitrogen, phosphorus, and potassium, the macronutrients plants need to thrive. You will see the N-P-K ratio listed on fertilizer packages.

Open-pollinated. Varieties that are not produced through hybridizing. Seeds from OP varieties saved and replanted from one season to the next will produce offspring with the same qualities as the parent plant.

Organic gardening. The basic definition: No use of pesticides and synthetic fertilizers. The big picture: Creating a balanced ecosystem in which soil, water, insects, and wildlife are nurtured and resources are replenished in their natural form.

Organic matter. Decaying plant residue, such as leaves, grass clippings and compost. It stimulates the activity of vital microbes in the soil.

Photoperiod. The amount of light vs. dark in the daily cycle that a plant is exposed to. Sometimes referred to as "day-length."

Pistil. A thin tube emerging from the female plant's ovaries which captures the pollen. A 'pistillate" plant is the scientific term for a female.

Sepal. One of the individual leaves of the calyx.

Sinsemilla. Cannabis produced without pollination, which therefore is seedless.

Stamen. The pollen-producing part of a plant. Scientists refer to male plants as "staminate."

Tetrahydrocannabinol. The psychoactive component of cannabis, THC (as it is commonly referred to) is produced by the plant and is believed to protect it against grazing animals.

Index